RETURNING to ONENESS

The SEVEN KEYS of ASCENSION

LESLIE TEMPLE-THURSTON
with BRAD LAUGHLIN

CoreLight Publishing
Santa Fe, New Mexico

For information:
CORELIGHT PUBLISHING
223 North Guadalupe Street, PMB 275
Santa Fe, NM 87501-1850
(888) 989-3552 (US/Canada)
(505) 424-8844 (Outside US/Canada)
Website: www.corelight.org
email: info@corelight.org

Cover painting: Augusta Lucas-Andreae
Augusta's art is available through CoreLight's online store.

Cover design, book design, and typography:
Kathleen Sparkes, White Hart Design, Albuquerque

Editor: Brad Laughlin

LCCN: 2002091941
ISBN: 0-9660182-9-X

ACKNOWLEDGMENTS

A special thank you to Victoria More, the instigator of this book project, whose joy, enthusiasm, inspiration, and assistance have been essential ingredients.

Thank you to all our friends who transcribed the original tapes of Leslie's talks on the seven keys: Terry McGill, Audrey Szabo, Kim Morgan, Ann Pettus, Chris McDonald, Catherine Shaw, Julia Hayden, Barbara Raimond, Julia Wolfe, and Sage Magdalene. We are deeply grateful for the time and energy you gave this project.

We offer our gratitude to Augusta Lucas-Andreae for her beautiful and appropriate painting that graces the cover of *Returning to Oneness*.

We truly appreciate Kathy Sparkes' talent for book design, her impeccability, and her heartfelt dedication.

We extend a big thank you to all of our friends who supported the book project in other ways: Ann Dales, Pam Costa, and Leslie Staller.

For Sananda

CONTENTS

PREFACE

The seven keys are simple, powerful, and invaluable tools to assist us on the path of spiritual awakening—especially in the wake of these turbulent, accelerated times in which we live. Leslie has brought forward these seven precious jewels of wisdom to help speed our journey of ascension in consciousness, moving us into greater states of heart-centeredness, forgiveness, compassion, and truth. The keys unlock the doorways between the chakras and allow a river of light to flow through the body, moving us into a conscious connectedness with our own inner divine nature, into the truth of who we are. They are a foundation for the teachings of non-duality and prepare us for living in unity consciousness in the body.

We have included at the end of each chapter in which one of the keys is presented a process, a prayer, and a meditation. These three practical exercises assist in grounding the teachings in a solid and tangible way. We suggest that you take the time to complete the three exercises before moving on to the next chapter in order to consolidate the understanding of each key.

As the keys were originally presented in a series of taped talks that Leslie gave over the course of two years, my role has been to compile and edit the transcripts of her talks and her writings, and to summarize our conversations. Leslie has also written some new material for this book, which was not presented in her original talks on the subject. I am deeply grateful for the opportunity to assist in bringing the seven keys forward. May you receive as much as I have from learning to use and live the seven keys of the ascension process.

Brad Laughlin
Santa Fe, New Mexico
April 26, 2002

FOREWORD

I remember well the first time I was introduced to the concept of the seven keys as a method to support ascension in consciousness. It was during a chilly winter morning, early in February of 2000. A group of five of us were sitting together in the silence of deep meditation. We were taking a break from our busy lives to spend the first part of the new millennium in stillness, sharing a silent meditation and contemplation retreat, nestled away in picturesque Santa Fe, New Mexico. During most of the month our friend and mentor, Leslie Temple-Thurston, watched over our progress as she periodically checked in from her own home a few blocks away. Now she had come to join us for the final few days of our retreat, to enjoy some rest herself and to mentor us in processing and integrating our experiences of the previous four weeks.

We were just settling into an early morning two-hour group meditation, when suddenly Leslie surprised us all by calling out, "Stop." This was unexpected. "Don't you feel the way you are all blocking the flow—right here?" She pointed to the area between, and a little bit above, her eyebrows. "Right here at the third eye, there's an energetic ceiling that you're hitting up against, and it's keeping you from opening to your full connection to source." It was true. There it was, so subtle as to be almost imperceptible, but oppressing us nonetheless. It was a sense of being held in check, of being blocked from the full, all-encompassing, exquisite experience of Oneness that we had all come to know in deep meditation. Using our will during meditation to get past the block did not seem to work. So, we decided to stop and investigate just what it was that was creating this stuck-ness in our consciousness.

What followed was an incredible four days as Leslie revealed five of the seven keys. We worked together to comprehend how to use them to open our awareness and to come into complete alignment with the Divine. Invariably, as we finished a group meditation, Leslie would be writing, trying to get the latest download of information concretized onto paper. Then we would process and investigate how the lock had been instituted, how we held it in the body, and how we could use the knowledge and understanding of the keys to unlock and unblock our awareness. We reviewed our stories and patterns about loss and gain, betrayal, faith, divine will, and our identification with the ego. We felt the power of these dramas and our attachment to them and were inspired by Leslie's own stories of how she had confronted and dealt with similar egoic patterning.

Over the subsequent weeks and months Leslie brought forward the two final keys. All of the information became more clarified and complete as she shared the knowledge with her students and with those who attended her public events. As a teacher of transformation, Leslie has a rare and wonderful gift, or "specialty" you could call it. In addition to giving public talks and *darshans*, she is an amazing mentor to those who are truly committed to their spiritual awakening, as she painstakingly guides them into deeper and more profound levels of self-inquiry and awareness of their own unique God-direct path. These keys are for everyone who has a passion for ascending and awakening into the fullness of who they are. They are a gift from Spirit, made available by a rare and wonderful being.

Victoria More
Santa Fe, New Mexico
April 29, 2002

THE
JOURNEY OF
ASCENSION

ASCENSION IS TALKED ABOUT A GREAT DEAL
NOWADAYS, yet it is still somewhat misunderstood
and also still seems to create confusion, even in
the minds of individuals actively seeking it. Just hearing
the word "ascension" used to evoke visions for some
people of motherships coming to the rescue, or the hand
of God coming down to lift us up sometime in the omi-
nous future when it was predicted that the going would
get tough. Seemingly to some, it was about being able to
escape from the harsh, cruel world that was to be our lot
when we reached the fast-approaching end times. Nowadays, since there is a greater receptivity to what ascension actually is, there is also a need to look more deeply
and realistically at it.

In fact the experience of ascension has been with us

for eons. And it is a very real, tangible, and immediate experience available to us right now, should we choose it—an experience completely connected to our physical life and body. Ascension is actually another term for the experience of awakening to the state of enlightenment— or unity consciousness—our highest potential. The misunderstandings around it exist because it is definitely a non-ordinary state, difficult to define, and as yet little understood in our ordinary world.

The word "ascension" is a very graphic and literal description of the journey to enlightenment, especially when viewed from the perspective of the anatomy of the subtle-physical body. This is because it describes the energetic journey on an ever-ascending path, up through the chakra levels from the root chakra to the crown chakra. While this is an inner energetic and bodily experience, it also depicts the complete transformation of our perceptions and experiences of the outer world around us.

Ascension through the chakra levels is also about individual consciousness moving from the ordinary, worldly state, which is a fairly slow vibration, to a higher and faster vibratory state, yet at the same time remaining solidly grounded. We venture forth from a judgmental, polarized, and limited mind, which keeps us susceptible to states of negativity at least half the time, to the experience of being liberated from negativity and limitation into the expanded, universal mind. It is in this state that we can realize our full potential as humans and experience more of the interconnectedness of all of life.

As we take this journey, we become beings of heart, living in compassion, generosity, and tremendous strength and wisdom. We are diving into the mystery of eternal beingness, yet simultaneously we are becoming more practical, grounded, and "real" as our consciousness becomes more based in truth. We are moving from an old, dysfunctional system into a new, more inclusive system, from the third-dimension into higher-dimensional consciousness, from a win–lose paradigm to a win–win paradigm.

The journey of ascension actually takes place right in the energy body. Our awareness is aligned in, and moves through, the energy body continuously, reflecting our shifting states of awareness. With every thought, emotion, and action, our awareness flows through the body, either ascending or descending our consciousness. Sometimes our awareness moves in a way that is harmonious with life and is aligned with our highest good. When it does, we feel fulfilled, alive, able to meet life with enthusiasm and optimism, ready to meet the world fully. Other times it moves erratically, seemingly out of synch with the rhythms of our natural flow, and we feel drained and depleted, as though we are wasting our energy. In this instance, we feel confused, thwarted by life's roadblocks, unable to fulfill our dreams, and we wonder what is going wrong.

In this book we take a detailed look at exactly how this works, at why consciousness sometimes moves in an erratic, draining way, and at how certain "locks," states of consciousness or thought-forms, which reside in the body, obstruct our natural flow of life force. The seven "keys" help to open those locks and restore the natural flow that is our birthright. We will use the subtle body and chakras as a map in order to explore how our consciousness moves through the body on the journey of ascension. But before we go there, let's look first at what ascension is not.

COMPLETING LIFE IN THE SEPARATE SYSTEM

Ascension does not mean leaving something behind, just walking out on, or abandoning the old system of consciousness. And this is a very important point to understand. Rather, it means completing the old system.

You cannot leave the old, third-dimensional system, a system of great disconnection and separation from one another and from other species, until you have completed all of the incomplete lessons that still await you there. The system of separation is an old way of perceiving, in which we see, feel, and believe that we are separate, autonomous entities, and that we are not connected to the outside world, to other people, and to God. All your unfinished business in the separate system will hold you back, and therefore you must attend to it. In the separate system we believe reality is the material world; we believe matter is what matters. We believe that what we can see and touch is real, and that what we cannot see or touch is not real.

All the stories about life that you still believe are real will be blind spots that suck you into a maelstrom of attraction and repulsion and negative and positive thinking, keeping you connected to the old, limited, dualistic, third-dimensional paradigm.

Since life is really about learning lessons, you cannot move on until you have learned them. When you have done so, you are free because you have incorporated, completed, and integrated the third dimension, and thus you move on.

Because of this very important fact, we must attend to clearing and deconstructing any states of mind and emotion that keep us attached to the old way. We must process all of our old issues, limiting beliefs and personality patterns that lock us into these limited states of consciousness.

Processing is a form of self-inquiry—a way of looking at our egoic self. "Ego" refers to the personality structure, which results from childhood and worldly conditioning. The term "to process" means to examine and to inquire deeply into the nature of our conditioned and unbalanced egoic programming with the intention of moving our awareness into balance and truth. We process our consciousness in order to become clear and ultimately to find our wholeness.

Processing the egoic programming is a very fast way of parting the veils of separation and refining our awareness to where we are not part of the old system any more, and begin to live in the open heart. Without that "seeing" of life's lessons, we have to live out those lessons in the physical world in the form of negative experiences. That can take years and cause much unnecessary suffering. The approach of processing the imbalances in the personality ties in with the old yogic instruction to be "in the world but not of it." *Arjuna*

PASSING THROUGH THE EYE OF THE NEEDLE

Your growth toward higher dimensional consciousness means a gradual dis-identification with your old reality and old identity. It is preparation for the journey through the eye the needle. The eye of the needle represents the doorway through which we pass when we allow our old reality to dissolve. Only the essential Self, the pure essence that you are, can pass through the eye of the needle, ascending into the next dimension. That essence is you, not as your personality, but as Oneness, and in that state of Oneness, you pass through the minute opening between the worlds and into the next dimension.

Thus the most important thing for us to attend to at this moment in time is our attachment to our old, third-dimensional personality programs. We can let go of attachments by deeply processing them, to where we are well and truly complete with all that the third dimension has to teach us. In this way we are actually decoding it to the point of becoming completely unplugged from it. We will then come to the place where we understand deeply that we are actually not the personality—that the old third-dimensional personality is a false self with which we are mistakenly identified, and that our true deeper nature is as the eternal Self.

The old third-dimensional system of separation is a certain bandwidth of vibratory frequency—a small part of the huge range of all the frequencies of creation. The ego is programmed to perceive only within that bandwidth. We, acting through the ego, are bound by its limitations. By seeing and transforming the old personality patterns, by letting them go and making new and different choices in our daily lives, we vastly increase the speed of our vibration to where our consciousness is no longer bound by the limitations of the old system. We begin to expand beyond it, into a new bandwidth.

Processing will wake us up to all the structures still rooted in the old way and bring us into a place of witnessing all the sides of this third-dimensional system that are still hidden from our sight in the unconscious. This will allow us to see where we are still hooking into it. Making the unconscious conscious is what the journey of ascension is all about.

Time is of the essence now for all of us as we approach the moment that has been predicted for the completion of this cycle, the year 2012, and processing becomes a very fast way to gain the understandings of our lessons. Completing the lessons allows the release of our attention from those places where we previously had blind spots.

The technique called "squares" that I teach in the book, *The Marriage of Spirit—Enlightened Living in Today's World*, is one method of processing, and it especially helps you see hidden sides of your old personality and thus awakens you to all the unconscious sides of the programs you run. Doing squares will also actually deconstruct the egoic programs as you finish them.

Using the seven keys presented in this book is also a powerful way of processing. In this accelerated time, you must have some method of processing the ego in order to stay on track with your path of transformation and spiritual awakening. Any way of processing that works for you is fine, as long as you do it regularly! You will not be able to ascend into "unity consciousness" and leave the old system without some proactive way of letting go and dissolving.

DUALITY

All the dualities that we hold in consciousness can be unified into the Oneness that is our origin and source, bringing us back to perceiving unity consciousness and allowing a tremendous speeding up of our vibration. In this world all individuals are holding varying degrees of separation in their patterning. How much separation someone experiences seems to depend on how much wounding he/she is carrying. Separation and wounding cause the vibration to be slower. Let's talk about duality for a moment so that you have an understanding of the dynamics that give rise to the slower, and also to the faster, vibrations—so that you understand how you can affect them.

This world is a world of duality. Because of the dual nature of our consciousness and our world—dual meaning divided in two—we perceive life in myriad pairs of opposites. Good and bad, pain and pleasure, joy and sadness, and life and death are just a few examples. There are many, many more pairs of opposites to which we are subject on a daily basis. Just a brief moment of reflection will reveal the truth of this.

Each person's egoic consciousness is programmed to exist within the context of all of life's pairs of opposites. The ego, or personality, is involved in all the pairs of opposites all the time. Life is dictated by our experiences of these states.

All the pairs of opposites are polarized by a magnetic field that holds them in a dynamic interplay with each other. The two sides of every pair spin around each other as a result of the magnetic force of attraction and repulsion. Since we are identified with the ego, this subjects us to the positives and negatives of all the states of mind and emotion in our bandwidth. In other words, in the third dimension we cannot experience the positive side of a pair of opposites without being subjected to the negative side at some point.

The motion caused by the magnetic field is an oscillation back and forth, operating like a pendulum. And the further apart the extremes of polarization are, the slower the vibration we will experience in our minds, emotions, and physical bodies.

This back-and-forth motion accounts for the mood changes that we experience in our daily lives. The ego balances itself by flip-flopping between negative and positive. However, this is a crazy, roller-coaster kind of balance and can be very stressful. It results in consciousness vibrating more slowly. Human life is stressed by living at a slower vibration because of the extremes of dark and light we experience. There is another way to find balance, a far less stressful way, and that is by unifying the pairs of opposites and coming back to our original state of unity. In other words, consciousness oscillates less and thus has a higher vibration. This allows the consciousness to ascend. Ascended paradigms vibrate at a faster speed.

It is not within the scope of this book to explore in any detail how the system of separation and duality works. But if you feel you need more information on the subject, a major portion of *The Marriage of Spirit— Enlightened Living in Today's World*, is dedicated to exploring it.

THE FLOW OF LIFE FORCE THROUGH THE BODY

We have many bodies other than the physical. Our complete, all-encompassing body is really a body of energy and consciousness. It comprises a mental body, an emotional body, and a vast light body as well. Our life force is always naturally flowing through, and animating all, of our bodies. When we choose to awaken to truth, a particularly powerful and vital flow of energy or light is activated in the body. In the East it is known as *kundalini*. It comes from the Sanskrit word, *kundal*, which means "coil." Seen clairvoyantly, kundalini is coiled at the base of the spine, like a snake, and when awakened, moves serpent-like up through the body. The natural flow is from the base of the spine, or the root chakra, to the top of the head, or the crown chakra. Before we proceed with our discussion of how this flow relates to the seven keys, let's take a brief look at the anatomy of the light body, also known as the subtle body or aura.

THE LIGHT BODY ANATOMY —
THE CHAKRAS

Chakras are energy centers in the body and are active at all times, whether we are conscious of them or not. *Chakra* is a Sanskrit word that denotes circle and movement, or it can be translated as "wheel." Chakras are associated with aspects of the physical, mental, and emotional bodies. We have many chakras within, and even some beyond, the physical body. There are seven main chakras in the body, and they are the ones we will address here.

There are aspects of consciousness and behavioral characteristics associated with each chakra. Often in meditating on the chakra, we can perceive the unique attributes of the consciousness associated with each chakra as described below. For the purposes of this book, we explore only the basic aspects of consciousness associated with each chakra; there are actually many more.

The first chakra is called the root chakra and is located between the anus and the genitals, at the base of the spine. The consciousness associated with the root chakra is that of security, physical survival, the fight-and-flight mechanism, and life-and-death struggles.

7TH CHAKRA
CROWN

6TH CHAKRA
THIRD EYE

5TH CHAKRA
THROAT

4TH CHAKRA
HEART

3RD CHAKRA
SOLAR PLEXUS

2ND CHAKRA
NAVEL

1ST
CHAKRA
ROOT

The chakras are energy centers in the subtle body. Seen clair-voyantly, the radiating rays resemble flowers or wheels. They are the interface between the subtle body and the physical body.

The second chakra is located on the front of the body between the navel and the genitals. Sexuality, pro-creation, creativity, the nurturing emotions, and family or tribal issues are associated with it.

The third chakra is located at the solar plexus. It is the power center and is where we work out dualistic issues of power–powerlessness—tyrant–victim, loss–gain, success–failure, and dominance, manipulation, and control. This is where we learn the lessons associated with polarized power, authority, name, fame, and all the shadow states associated with power, such as rejection, betrayal, and abandonment.

The fourth chakra is located in the middle of the chest and is often called the heart chakra. The consciousness associated with the heart chakra is that of love, faith, devotion, duty, and compassion. It is also associated with the ins and outs of love relationships—rejection and acceptance.

The fifth chakra is located at the throat, and is the energy center of the voice, expression, artistry, knowledge, mastery, and will.

The sixth chakra is located between the eyebrows and is known as the third eye. This is the energy center of conscience, wisdom, insight, clairvoyance, psychic perception, and multi-dimensionality.

The seventh chakra is located at the top of the head, and is known as the crown chakra because it sits on the head like a crown. It is a vortex of energy that opens upward like a funnel. The royal crown that kings and queens wear is a representation of it in physical form. Also known as the thousand-petaled lotus, the crown chakra is associated with our sense of connectedness to All That Is and, at its deepest level, with our union with the Divine within us.

It is easier to experience our natural state of non-duality or Oneness in the upper chakras, especially in the crown. Many people make the mistake of thinking that by keeping their awareness in the upper chakras they are free of the third dimension, and they "train" themselves not to go down into the lower chakras with their conscious awareness. By opening your crown chakra, which you can do just by willing it open in meditation, you can temporarily experience a unified state. But the problem is that the crown does not automatically stay open once you have opened it with your will. Because of the programming of polarization in the egoic mind, the crown chakra closes again as soon as you forget to hold it open. Then awareness drops back into the programming and loses that open state. So training yourself to stay in the upper chakras will not bring you to freedom from ego.

Trying to remain in the consciousness of only the upper chakras is the practice of avoidance and denial. When we indulge in avoidance and denial of the third-dimensional worldly consciousness of the lower three chakras, the awareness is still trapped there from childhood programming, and it is simply being kept unconscious. It has not been cleared and deconstructed.

It is important to know that at the deepest level of the subtle body, unified consciousness resides in the body all the way down to the root, not just in the crown and upper chakras. As you use the keys, especially clearing the first, second, and third chakras of their shadow content, you will experience unity consciousness all the way down to your root chakra. Eventually your crown and your root will be emanating the same unified state. There will be no difference between them. So forget about the idea that to live in unity consciousness you have to reside only in the crown and upper chakras. It just is not so.

Awakening to the inherent unity in the lower chakras is immanently possible. It does take a little longer and require more dedication, however, because it means being willing to face the egoic shadow.

THE LIGHT BODY ANATOMY — THE CORE

The light body has a core or central axis from which the chakras emerge. In Sanskrit the core is known as the *shushumna*, and it corresponds roughly to the physical spine. The shushumna is a pathway of light. It is the luminous core of enlightenment within each one of us. It is the center of the cosmos, and is known in the Bible as the Tree of Life, one of its many names. Its "branches" of energy or light spread into all the different dimensional facets of all of the bodies.

Most people in the separate system are unaware that the core exists and rarely feel it. All the veils of the conditioned personality—fears, imbalances, negative and limiting belief systems, and so forth—have been wrapped

The shushumna or core (body's axis)

tightly around it and have hidden it from our conscious view. In fact, they resemble a coating of thick, black leather, like a sleeve, around the core. Between the chakras are locks where the veils constrict and cut off the flow of light and energy through our physical body. The illuminating flow of kundalini, once liberated, moves up and opens the locks to reveal the emanation of unity consciousness from the core. The locks limit the quantity of light we can access, thus keeping us in a limited system. As we ascend in vibration and let go of the beliefs in separation and limitation, the kundalini opens the locks and sweeps away the veils. We become conscious of the kundalini ascending, of the light of unity emanating from the core and of being connected all the way up, from root to crown chakra.

When a single, thread-like flow of light, or kundalini, ascends all the way up the core from root to crown, uninterrupted by egoic limitation, we begin to experience unity consciousness. In Sanskrit it is a state known as *samadhi*. The Christian Church refers to it as "the peace which passeth all understanding." As we clear the constricting, limiting locks in egoic consciousness and as we progress on the path of Self-discovery, the thread widens and our samadhi state evolves and grows. Samadhi is an actual experience of the light of the core and is an awakening to the knowledge of the cosmos—the beginning of enlightenment and of being "ascended."

Transcendental light is unified consciousness and contains information. When we enter samadhi, we download the information in the light, or unity consciousness, and later it is decoded through the mental body, where we become conscious of multidimensional understandings. For example, we may gain insights into a current process that would help to unravel a destructive behavior pattern, like overeating or smoking. Many of the world's great scientists, artists, and leaders have access to higher realms of light—whether consciously or unconsciously—and therefore they are able to receive information and brilliant new ideas in this way. Transcendental light is sometimes experienced—usually in meditation—as a blissful, ecstatic, ever-expanding presence; it is the unconditional love of the Divine.

The light of the core is experienced as unified or non-dual awareness—divine presence within us. Traditionally, developing awareness of the core is done mainly with meditation practice. With meditation, doorways gradually open in one's interior space, and the consciousness is flooded with the state of non-dual awareness that is our natural state.

Using the seven keys and other processing techniques to unravel knotted patterns and imbalances in the ego also allows us to thin out the veils. The non-dual awareness seeps through and realigns the ordinary everyday awareness, bringing us very easily and gently into a wonderfully integrated state of awakeness.

CHOOSING TO LOVE AT ALL TIMES

Since we are surrendering to the journey into and up the core, through all the levels of the third dimension, our first stop will be the fourth dimension where our consciousness begins to be centered more in the heart.

This means shifting into a love-based state from a power- or fear-based state.

Daily we must make the choice to love even if we do not understand how it will look. Even in the face of all of our tribulations and fears about change, we must let go more and more of all our power and control issues, which bind us to the third dimension.

In choosing love over power or fear, we will pass through the eye of the needle into the pathway to the next dimension. The pathway is the river of light, the core, and we are carried along on its current and reborn once again into the heart space. By choosing love, we are reborn into our own true and permanent heart presence. When we live life centered in the third chakra, the heart presence is hidden from our view.

When you choose love and let go of the old way, you may not be completely aware of the change this institutes. It can feel scary, and you may balk since it feels as though you are entering the unknown, folding your wings and going into free fall. If you react to the fear by buying into it, you will resist the process, and it will not happen. You will be unable to let go and experience the shift. Instead, you will fall back into the negative side of the third dimension and be stuck there, until the next time the choice between love and fear, or love and power, comes up. However, do not be concerned. The choice could come up the very next day since we are each making choices that decide our level of consciousness moment by moment. These choices are coming up constantly in subtle ways. Letting go is a very important part of the path of love; and be assured, it gets easier with practice.

As you enter the eye of the needle even momentarily, you become pure beingness, nothing but light in fact. In our egoic self we are used to feeling like we are "somebody" or even its polarity on some days, "nobody." This doorway into the heart is about passing between these two sides of the ego and momentarily becoming who you truly are, pure beingness, energy without any human attributes.

THE SEQUENCE OF THE KEYS

The keys are presented in a unique sequence, rather than in the order of the chakra numbers. It is a mystical order that most easily expedites the unlocking of the doorways between the chakra levels. It is best to learn the keys in the order they are presented here and initially to use them in this order. With time you will become very familiar with each of them. Once you have learned them, you can use them in a free-form way in any order you wish. The following two pages include a diagram and a list of the seven keys.

THE SEVEN KEYS OF ASCENSION

THE FIRST KEY:
Do not believe in loss or gain
(between the 5th and 6th chakras)

THE SECOND KEY:
Forgive all betrayals
(between the 3rd and 4th chakras)

THE THIRD KEY:
Not my will but Thine
(between the 4th and 5th chakras)

THE FOURTH KEY:
Have faith in the support of the invisible realms
(between the 1st and 2nd chakras)

THE FIFTH KEY:
View the ego impersonally
(between the 2nd and 3rd chakras)

THE SIXTH KEY:
Accept your death
(just below the 1st chakra)

THE SEVENTH KEY:
Accept your divinity
(between the 6th and 7th chakras)

7TH KEY
Accept your divinity

1ST KEY
Do not believe in
loss or gain

3RD KEY
Not my will
but Thine

2ND KEY
Forgive all
betrayals

5TH KEY
View the ego
impersonally

6TH KEY
Accept your
death

4TH KEY
Have faith
in the support
of the invisible
realms

THE
FIRST KEY

DO NOT
BELIEVE IN
LOSS OR GAIN

"DO NOT BELIEVE IN LOSS OR GAIN" IS OUR FIRST
KEY, and it opens the lock between the throat
chakra (fifth) and the third-eye chakra (sixth).
Crucial to our understanding here is not to believe the
egoic programming about loss, and of course it also involves not believing in its opposite, gain, either. Loss and
gain are a polarized duality and are inseparable.

Now you may truly believe that there is such a
thing as loss and gain, and in the old reality it certainly
appears to be true—that is, "seeing is believing." Yet the
truth of our eternal beingness is that nothing can be
added to us that is not already there, and conversely
nothing can be taken away from who we already are. We
are perfect, complete, and absolutely whole. When we
know this truth, we are in our most natural state.

The idea of loss and gain is a program held in the matrix of third-dimensional egoic programming, and in a sense is nothing more than an idea held in the limited mind. Therefore it is essential on the path of Self-discovery to clear the shadow of loss and gain to find liberation from the third dimension.

Let's look at this key in terms of our schematic of the subtle body. Our consciousness naturally perceives interconnectedness and ultimately unity consciousness at the third eye and above, at the crown chakra. This is in addition to finding it in the core—should we be able to enter there. Below the third eye, and down through the chakras, the ego perceives duality. This is where the third eye, the one single eye, located roughly between the eyebrows, becomes the two—the dual physical eyes. This spot between the third eye and the two physical eyes is the origin of our *either–or* mind, the mind that flip-flops from one side of a polarity to the other. In this spot, below the third eye, subtle meridians of energy begin—upward and downward flows of awareness from which we perceive duality. They rotate around, in a double-helix, surrounding and veiling the core. Here, awareness is deceived into the program of extreme polarization of the third dimension, and our true, eternal perceiver becomes veiled and clouded.

In Matthew 6:22, Jesus said, "If therefore thine eye be single, thy whole body shall be full of light." He was referring to the fact that when our flow of awareness ascends permanently to the third eye, becoming established there, then not only does the body become filled with energy manifesting as light, but when it is vibrating fast enough, we become illumined and permanently conscious of our true nature as unity.

CHARLIE BROWN'S CHRISTMAS TREE

Loss is only a perception of the limited mind. One year in the early 1980s I had worked quite late on Christmas Eve and had to drive a couple of hours down the Interstate to my apartment. Although I had never spent Christmas alone, due to my circumstances that year, I was destined to be spending Christmas on my own and had done nothing about it—made no preparations or anything. I had no furniture either, since I had just moved into the apartment. Somehow it felt like I was being set up to have quite possibly a most depressing holiday. Even though it was late, I thought, "Well, I'll just go down to the local Christmas tree lot and see if I can get a tree." It was already 8:30 p.m. The attendant was closing the gate as I got there, and the lot was empty of people and trees. I realized that all the tree shoppers must be at home eating Christmas Eve dinner with their families and friends. The salesman didn't really have anything left, but we found a nice branch. Under the circumstances I was *thrilled* to get the branch! I took it home and sort of propped it up in the corner. It crossed my mind that this was going to be a dreary Christmas since

I had no decorations, just a very short string of rainbow-colored lights, which I wound around the tree. On the journey home, the branch had transformed in my mind into a tree. It was a Charlie Brown Christmas tree. I made the conscious choice not to feel like a "loser," and not to feel depressed about being alone in an empty apartment during Christmas. Instead of buying into the idea of loss, I chose to perceive my circumstances differently.

To my surprise I soon became totally entranced by the small tree/branch with its colored lights. It lit up the whole place since there was no furniture to compete with it. So I sat for hours in meditation—open-eyed meditation, just gazing at this tree. And I ended up sitting the whole night. Given that it was Christmas Eve, I thought, "Well, this is probably a good time to meditate all night." During the long hours all I did was sing the praises of the Divine and express my gratitude, giving thanks for the year that had gone by and for the blessings of my life. I focused on all the wonderful things that had happened, and I *loved this tree*. I just worshipped the Divine through the beauty of this Charlie Brown tree!

I think it was about 1:00 a.m., when an energy came in that was so transcendental that I couldn't focus properly on the lights anymore. My eyes went out of focus so that the lights were refracting in every direction, and the tree became sort of kaleidoscopic, rainbow-cloaked, and aura-enclosed—just exquisite. All I could see was the aura around the lights and these rainbow beams going everywhere. It got more and more beautiful as the night flowed on. My state of consciousness became increasingly vast, eternal, and transcendental. The experience lasted through the whole of the next day.

That day I walked on the deserted beach near my home and was in ecstasy. It didn't matter that my tree was this little Charlie Brown branch and that I had five colored lights on it. It had turned into a magical doorway into eternity. I was tapping into the generosity of spirit. With this experience came the realization that, "When you are in equanimity with the Truth, what will manifest for you is beyond your wildest dreams."

LOSS MEANS LOSS OF ENERGY

When the ego feels it has suffered a loss, the mental, emotional, and physical bodies contract and lose their light. They become deprived of energy, or life force. This loss of life force brings up deep-seated fears in the ego that make it react with certain behaviors, such as the need to defend and protect itself from further loss.

At the very root of the loss of life force lies the fear of death. When the egoic mind extrapolates extreme loss of life force, it feels death approaching. For within the limited knowledge of the ego, the total loss of life force equals the total loss of everything. The ego fears loss because only it can die. Who "you" truly are, can never die.

Overall, the consciousness of the third dimension is based on loss and gain. Experiencing loss drops awareness out of the natural unified state, which, unbeknownst to us, we are in more than we realize, mostly when we feel contentment or peace. It does not matter if it is a big loss or a small loss. Big and small are relative perceptions of the limited, egoic mind.

Watch how your mind will immediately pick up on a thought that has the kernel of loss woven into it. The mind is hyper-vigilant about loss; it is watching constantly for signs of potential losses. Observe how thoughts that even hint at the possibility of loss drop your awareness into exhaustion—loss of energy. Loss is not only associated with material possessions or the loss of loved ones in relationships; there are many other kinds of loss. Some examples of loss would be: disapproval, criticism, blame, rejection, betrayal, abandonment, self-doubt, lack of self-esteem, withholdings, and grievances. Loss can be so many things on so many levels: loss of face, of dignity, of energy, of happiness, of connectedness, of resources, of inspiration, of your divine state, and so forth. There are many more. In fact, any experience of the negative side of any duality would contain a tonality of loss.

Perhaps you can't find your toothbrush, and it is making you crazy. It is a small loss, but it is enough to spin you. Sometimes the polarized mind can even make the loss of your toothbrush into a betrayal by God and drop you right down into feeling a state of deep separation! And then of course there are the other, big losses that seem more life shattering, and are very obviously energy draining. So it is important to observe how the egoic mind plays tricks on your awareness and sets you up to lose energy.

The Witness

It is important to develop a strong, neutral witness in this clearing work. The witness is that part of you that is outside the ego—outside the spin of negative and positive polarities. The stronger your ability to be in the witness, observing life from the neutral place outside of the ego, the better your ability to clear egoic shadow issues.

As you learn to identify more deeply with the witness, you will have an ever-increasing ability to recognize all the facets of your egoic programming. The witness is fully centered at all times and occupies the middle ground between the extremes of negative and positive. Since this is so, it recognizes that ego is involved when the intense fears associated with loss come up. Likewise, it also recognizes that ego is involved when the intense desires associated with gain come up. It has a moderating, stabilizing, and balancing influence on the ego's dance between the fear of loss and the desire for gain.

A strong witness is most important when we work on patterns that involve the issue of loss. When a situation arises that sparks excessive reactivity, the witness can recognize it. The witness knows that excessive reactivity to something means that childhood or infant issues are involved. You might find yourself thinking, "Gosh, I'm a grownup person. Why am I feeling like this?" The witness knows that doing the shadow-clearing work involves slipping in and out of our infant issues constantly.

THE DEPRIVED CHILD

The ego's first programming with loss begins to be instituted in infancy. Therefore in working with healing our patterns around loss, we must be willing to go back in time and look at our childhoods and even our infancies. Looking at the early programming around loss usually reveals the presence of a deprived child who lives inside us even when we are adults.

It is always important when working with a pattern to look at its opposite. The deprived child can have a number of opposites. One of them is a persona that takes the form of a greedy and power-hungry go-getter. The third-dimensional world is largely run by this polarity. The "black-hole" neediness of the deprived child and the resulting "hungry-ghost" greediness that develops in the adult are juxtaposed to form a very dominant personality structure.

The deprived child can grow up with other compensatory patterns too, such as someone who sublimates

compen-sation

his/her own neediness into finding fulfillment in serving others in a codependent way—the rescuer or the savior. In my observation there are four specific compensating overlays to the deprived child: the needy victim, the greedy tyrant, the withholding rebel, and the martyred savior. And each of these overlays will differ slightly through being held in either a feminine or masculine ego.

The neediness of the deprived child lends fire to the adult's compensatory behaviors. The adult feels the need to fill up the inner emptiness of loss and emotional deprivation through his/her own efforts. I call the one who efforts "the doer"—someone with an aggressive, driven quality that out-pictures as an often insatiable thirst to be somebody, in order to heal the nobody that the deprived child feels itself to be.

This hungry quality can appear as extreme rapacious greed, dominating and exploiting in its efforts to feel less like a loser, or it can also be a desire to succeed in somewhat more modest ways without the extreme abuse of power of the tyrant. The degree of compensating by the adult persona is proportional to the degree of wounding experienced by the deprived child.

One thing is robustly clear, the ambitious desire to fill oneself with material success will always fail—material success may come, but it will not satisfy the inner neediness. The program of the deprived child is a bottomless pit that can never be filled by the adult doer's compensating efforts. Yet we just have to look at the seductive material world around us to see that billions of people are deluded into believing that it might. However, it is a program, like a computer program, coded to give a result of emptiness. No matter how much material success is poured into the black hole of neediness, it cannot and never will feel fulfilled. Nothing short of the full healing of the inner deprived child will allow the adult to find fulfillment.

The egoic programming of the human ego can be very easily likened to a computer program. It can only do what it is programmed to do, unlike our true Self, which has awareness directly plugged into the unfathomable intelligence of universal mind. And because the deprived-child program is designed to produce a result of emptiness and loss, then that is what it produces. Indeed, that is all it can produce. It can *never* give a reading of fulfillment—leaving the hungry, greedy go-getter forever attempting to override the "empty" program by creating a "full" program, which is an act of futility. The only solution is to see the empty and full programs as forming a polarity in ego and to do the processing work to dissolve them.

BEYOND LOSS AND GAIN IS LOVE

Love has the capacity to multiply itself. It has a mysterious component in that it always multiplies itself, and it never divides. This is an important thing to remember about love. Material things, when separated from the component of love, have a way of dividing themselves. If you cut an apple in half and give half away, your material eyes will see that you have only half an apple left. Your material eyes are the dual, physical eyes that choose to run things through the filters of loss and gain.

But when you give love, whether the love takes the form of a generous gift of material things, or of energy, such as prayer or plain old goodwill, then that love multiplies, and the energy exchange does not involve loss and gain. If you give away material things on a flow of love, the material things will multiply, too. It is the love that multiplies them.

If you are feeling love, even if it is just for five minutes in the middle of some working day, stop and watch how all-encompassing it is. It connects and contains. Send it out in the form of gratitude, appreciation, and wishes for others to receive the gift of the grace that you are enjoying in that moment. Just let your heart create the intention, and the love will do its work of multiplication.

When you suffer a loss, it is the relative mind that says, "This wasn't supposed to happen. I don't deserve this." If instead, you can find the heart and say, "God's grace gave me this experience, and I accept it with an even mind," then the soul will take a quantum leap forward.

When you choose to buy into loss, disappointment can take over and ruin your day. Choosing not to buy into the loss allows you to see life's grace gently guiding you through the necessary changes toward truth, to seeing a bigger picture. As it happens, allow yourself to understand that there is a lesson being given to you that will free you. In that freedom you will find the grace to express gratitude for the growth taking place in you.

This is how compassion is born in us. You can have compassion for yourself, as you would for others, for the wounding and the losses that you appear to have taken.

DECODING THE LOSS MATRIX

The training the first key offers us is this: to give up the notion that we are locked into this little loss-gain reality and its ongoing tragedy and suffering. There are brilliant, vast forces at work at a soul level which are eternal and infinite. [These forces are bringing us through wondrous experiences that evolve us.] They are not out to harm us.] They are only here to help us grow. And the experiences do help us grow when we do not run them through the old programming of loss and gain. The quality of our lives is defined by what we focus on in each moment. Using this key helps us to focus moment to moment on the big picture, rather than on the small, limiting idea of loss or gain.

By being alert and conscious of the mental ideas and beliefs that arise in the mind, we can witness the mind creating the events of our lives. We can use these moments of clarity to choose whether or not to be in relativity— for example, relating to loss and gain.

If our witness catches the mind fearing loss on a mental or emotional level, we will not necessarily have to learn the lesson of loss as a physical experience by living it out in the world. By inquiring into what the mind is doing, by immediately detaching from the fear, and by facing the unknown that the situation presents, we can discern the lesson on the mental or emotional level, which is a quicker, less painful way than having the issue manifest on a physical level.

Here is an example of how this works. I once worked with a woman who asked me to help her process her fear of losing her friends. Her childhood wounding was deep, and she complained that nobody liked her. She was lonely and depressed because she would make friends and always lose them. She knew she was somehow pushing them away, but could not fix the problem. We looked at her fear of losing her friends and processed the childhood wounding. Among other issues, we processed her neediness, which grew out of a dysfunctional relationship with her mother. Her deep desire for friends was so extreme that her newfound friends were repulsed by the neediness and would leave shortly after meeting her. With processing, it was not long before she cleared deep layers of victim patterning and much of the compensatory behaviors associated with it. Her neediness dissipated. As a result, she became less afraid of losing friends. Her ability to witness her fear pattern strengthened. She developed the ability to catch the fear in her mind in the moment and not to buy into it. Now she has plenty of friends because she deconstructed much of the childhood programming that caused her to be so desperate and grasping. She learned the lesson at a mental-emotional level through the processing, and so she does not have to live it out anymore on a physical level by actually gaining and losing friends. She is a much happier person now, her life is smoother, and she has more equanimity and detachment.

Everybody, whether they are witnessing or not, whether they are on an advanced spiritual path or not, is making choices in the mind, in each moment. Even though our egos run the programming of loss, there is always an opportunity in every moment to choose not to buy into it. And that is the process of ascension—not buying into the programming.

LETTING GO OF LOSS

Often we come up against some barriers in consciousness where parts of the ego just cannot let go. The ego simply will not release the losses that we believe we have taken in our life. The ego has made the losses a big deal or has found a pay off in some way. There is something we get from holding onto them, some way in which life reciprocates our sense of loss and deprivation. Everything is in the eye of the perceiver, however. We can choose to perceive differently.

If the losses have programmed the ego to feel inadequate, worthless, useless, or deprived, or have somehow robbed you of your dignity, it is very hard to let go of the negative image of yourself. There is also the positive side, though. This is where you feel self-importance and work really hard at trying to build self-esteem and confidence to help you feel good about yourself. It is important to remember that this positive side is all just ego, too. Old stories you have woven around losses and gains are all just aspects of the false personality, the false you. Dissolution is possible if you are willing to take a look at both the negative and the positive images that you hold about yourself and to realize that it is all egoic programming, not who you really are as eternal beingness.

Start by doing some in-depth exploring. Ask yourself, "What is this negative image I have of myself? What is the positive one?" Look at both of them and write about them in your journal. If you cannot see the negative one, delineate the positive one, because it will be the logical opposite.

Situations in life will trigger feelings of inadequacy, insecurity, or inferiority, which are basically feelings of loss. Even though something outside you may trigger the program holding those feelings, it is not the outside doing it to you. Never ever! It is coming from your inner programming of the deprived child.

Almost everyone feels inadequate, inferior, and

useless at least some of the time. It is because that old vibratory field of the deprived child is around your body all the time, as a miasma, a veil, even when you are not focused on it. It may be mostly unconscious, while its opposite, the positive side—superiority, for example—is mostly in the conscious awareness. Then the inadequacy and the superiority flip sides when something seemingly outside triggers a reaction.

It is important to try to define the vibratory fields associated with egoic states that you hold around your body. If you can feel them and give words to them in your journal, you are taking the first step toward a major clearing.

For example, as you explore your feelings, you may find words like incompetent, useless, insecure, shy, fearful, and damaged. Then you look for the antonyms of those words. For example: competent, useful, secure, outgoing, courageous, and healthy. As you make the lists of opposites, it is important to remember that none of it is you. It is not who you truly are as the Self. It is simply the programmed personality. Even if you have held onto it for 50 years, you do not have to for another 50 years.

Once you have felt the vibrations and witnessed them, you can say, "I choose not to carry this field around with me." Because you have found both the positive and negative sides of the ego, both the conscious and the unconscious, you can offer up both sides to Spirit in a prayer, releasing any attachment to both sides. As you do this, you can consciously choose not to buy into or believe the situation of loss that gave rise to the feelings. You may still have the memory in your mind, but this process will help diffuse the memory and take away the sting. In this way you can let the memory and the miasma go. They are not you.

THE EGO EXPANDS AND CONTRACTS WITH LOSS AND GAIN

Usually there is an enormous fear in the ego of what is beyond it. This is perceived as emptiness. The ego would rather hold onto negative baggage than actually let go and venture forth into this true, pristine state of beingness. The reason is that we project the fear of emptiness and of voidness onto the true void of eternity because that is all the ego knows. In our conditioned state, we do not know what the shining void of eternity is, unless we have had an experience of it in meditation or in some other context. The ego will fear it because it fears the unknown.

It is the ego's program to fear the unknown, because it sees its death. The ego fears its death. It would rather live in extreme states of limitation and even negativity than give up its power and let go—which means ego death. There is logic to that. When you are in a negative state, the egoic consciousness contracts, and in that contracting you find a feeling of security. In the comfort of contraction, you know you exist. There is no danger of your flying off like a helium balloon into outer space, which it sometimes feels could happen when the anchoring of the ego begins to dissipate. As a result the ego imagines and fears the helium balloon scenario.

The ego has the extremes of its negative side and its positive side, based on expansion and contraction. When it is negative, it contracts. It contracts to make itself dense and heavy, and that grounds it. If it contracts too much, then one starts feeling so dense that it becomes unbearable. So there is a lower limit to how much contraction the egoic programming will allow before it turns into its opposite. The energy moves in a figure eight. You go down into the negative, and when you hit the bottom extreme, you create a ray of hope, which moves it in the direction of expansion. Then up it goes and begins to expand again. Then the fear of floating off into the void comes in, and you will create a doubt, which institutes a contraction. This is the way the ego works, continuously cycling around, expanding and contracting.

Beyond the ego is simply beingness—changeless, eternal, complete, full, and luminous. To experience this beingness, we must release some of the ego's ballast. Ballast is a shipping term which means to weight down and stabilize. When a boat goes out to sea with no cargo, it will take on water just to keep it weighted down. Normally the cargo keeps the ship steady and weighted down in the water, but if the ship is too light, it bobs too much and can capsize. Like ships, we use our negative states to weight ourselves down and to stabilize. The ego believes it can become unstable, and of course, beliefs fulfill themselves.

So the egoic expansion and contraction can become unstable. But the real you, the perceiver, the eternal I, can never be unstable. Nothing can destabilize that. It is perfectly formed in what it is. It cannot change. It cannot lose anything, and it cannot gain anything. It has and is everything. Nothing can be added to it, and nothing can be taken away.

It is not possible to let go of all the ballast at once. It takes time. When you make a choice to let go of some of your ballast, there has to be a period of rewiring. The subtle meridians and all the circuits of the body get reconfigured in such a way that allows you to be able to hold the clear light of reality and you will find yourself evolving into a new state. The clear light of reality, the sense of stability and the permanent, changeless state of beingness, must be wired into the subtle bodies gradually, so that this cycling around the figure eight is minimal.

In the beginning it is the daily experience of the cycling ego that dominates our awareness, and as we make the choices to wake up to that and to see the truth, the amount of our attention that is caught in that figure eight diminishes. More of our attention will be held in the clear perceiver, and this is the process that happens within time.

So letting go of the idea of loss is first. We get it on a mental level first because mental energy is quick; it grasps things. Second is the emotional letting go, which is more challenging. Those vibratory fields that are our emotional states, which we hold in and around the body—feelings of confusion, disappointment, dissatisfaction, and despair, to name a few—are states that give us ballast. Remember to witness them. Remember, too, that you will not float into space if you let go of your negative emotional baggage. And remember your wholeness.

As you let go of the negativity, the cargo you take on is love. I suggest that you dedicate 365 days a year to remembering love. Never let a single day go by that you do not think of and honor your own ability to love and give love. Try each day to consciously make a point of expressing that love, feeling it inside yourself and expressing it in some way to somebody. If you can do that daily, then you will find you can do it the rest of your life. And you will be very happy. That is the key to happiness.

A Process

The following egoic clearing technique is called "polarity processing" and is explained in more detail in the book, *The Marriage of Spirit—Enlightened Living in Today's World.*

Write a story in your journal about an experience of loss. Be sure to include all your feelings about it. Don't economize with the paper. Be as thorough as you possibly can. Include things like: How do you fear loss? Is there any payoff in experiencing loss? How and why might you attract loss? How do you try to avoid loss? Go back through the story and circle all the descriptive words and phrases—adjectives, adverbs, anything with a charge to it. Make a list of all those circled words and phrases down the left-hand column of a page. Then in the right-hand column, write the opposites. These two lists are the polarities that comprise the ego, that lock you into attractions and repulsions and that keep you stuck in the limitation and duality of the separate system. Make an offering of the list and give it all back to Spirit. Let it all go, knowing none of it is who you truly are. You are eternity. In a meditation, release it, do not believe in the loss or the gain, try instead to feel love and compassion, and try to feel the movement of energy into the third eye.

A PRAYER

Oh Eternity, please take all of these states of mind which are unbalanced in this pattern and balance and clear them. Do this so that I may see more clearly and find my way home more easily. I offer up the egoic belief in loss and gain, and I ask to live more in love, compassion, and unity consciousness. I give thanks knowing this work will be done.

A Meditation

Sit comfortably. Take five or seven deep breaths until your breathing becomes calm and deep. Now visualize the core as it is situated along the central axis of the body. It looks rather like a luminous fluorescent tube running down the center of your subtle body. In the physical body it corresponds more or less to the spine but sits slightly in front of it. By visualizing it, you begin to feel its presence.

Imagine that you, as your essential Self, are the core. Think of how we write the letter "I," a straight vertical column. It means us—who we are. The letter "I," describing who we are, comes from the shape of the core. It is the most powerful energy meridian in all the bodies, and it is actually the "I." It is where the presence of the "I am-ness" is situated in us. At the same time it is also situated at the very center of the cosmos. It is not to be confused with the "I am something in particular," such as "I am a loser," "I am an artist," or "I am tall with brown eyes."

Sit with your attention on the core, holding center and feel your "I am-ness" for a while.

THE
SECOND KEY
FORGIVE ALL
BETRAYALS

FORGIVING ALL THE BETRAYALS OF LIFE IS THE SECOND KEY. This means all the betrayals that you have perpetrated on others, those that have been done to you, self-betrayals, and even those that you may have caused others to do to someone else.

Betrayal concerns the lock between the third chakra and the fourth chakra, between the solar plexus and the heart. This lock is a complex knot right on the diaphragm. As we seek to raise the kundalini energy up into the heart chakra, it cannot pass easily through this knot because the core is very tightly veiled here. The energy dams up, circulating instead in the abdomen, unable to make it into the heart. As we use this key and do the processing work, we are able to loosen and eventually untie this knot. In the East it is known as *the knot of Vishnu*. When it opened for me, my guides called it "Heaven's Gate." Forgiveness will open it. The vibration of forgiveness actually dissolves the hard knot and releases the contraction, so the energy can get through to your heart. It takes more than a one-time forgiveness and is more like learning to live in a continuous state of forgiveness.

Having an experience of betrayal means that we are identified with the egoic personality programs that are telling us that we are being let down, taking a loss, experiencing a breach of trust or feeling victimized by something. When we feel as though we deserve to have our needs met, and it is not happening, we feel betrayal. Life, from our third-dimensional perspective, has a tendency to dish out both major and minor betrayals.

The diaphragm is one of the main places where we hold our energy in contraction because of childhood wounding—wounding based on betrayal. As you clear and release feelings of betrayal and loss, you may find the diaphragm area softening. It is releasing tension and tightness. The diaphragm is the first muscle that begins contracting in the body of a newborn baby. When babies cry and scream and sob, it is the diaphragm that is working and beginning to tense and contract. So, much of our early childhood losses are stored in the diaphragm area. Tension in the diaphragm area blocks the kundalini energy from flowing freely into the heart chakra, preventing us from accessing the higher emotions such as forgiveness, tolerance, acceptance, and joy. Thus, as long as the early childhood wounding remains in place, we are unable to love as much as we are capable of—with far-reaching ramifications to our lives. As we begin to work on forgiving betrayals, the diaphragm plays a big part in the releasing associated with this key, indicating that it is the infant particularly that holds on to resentment, grudges, and old wounding. This is mainly because most infant programming has been forgotten.

So our focus for this chapter is moving beyond victim consciousness, which is perhaps the biggest issue facing humanity at this time. Victim consciousness and its opposite, the tyrant, are holding the whole world back from ascending into the new paradigm of heart-centered consciousness. As we unlock the betrayal knot associated with victim consciousness, we take a giant step forward in moving beyond the polarities of victim–tyrant, of power–powerlessness, of win–lose, and into the paradigm of love and of win–win consciousness.

The thick, rubbery muscle of the diaphragm, separating the chest from the abdomen, is the physical representation of the density of the consciousness that keeps the two paradigms separate. It acts as a barrier between the lower three chakras which are associated with worldly consciousness, and the upper four chakras which are associated more with our spiritual nature, with unified awareness, or with higher vibratory consciousness.

MEDITATE ON FORGIVENESS

It is important to meditate on forgiveness. See what you can forgive and what you cannot forgive. And if you cannot forgive, why not. If there is something you cannot forgive, you may see that the surface consciousness is in self-pity and that the shadow perceives something else. It may say something like, "A terrible betrayal happened to me, and I'm not going to believe that it didn't or that I caused it myself." There is often some sort of hook in consciousness here that is reluctant to give up on the grudge and the withholding. It feels it needs the shadow, has to have it. It may feel that it would rather die than give up the cherished notion of its suffering and of what it thinks it should have. It plans on holding on to the shadow until it has its needs met.

From the ego's perspective, forgiveness often comes down to forgiving God for causing us pain and suffering and for creating this world to be a place of pain and suffering. I use the word "God" here because even God when viewed from this level is seen as an outside persecutor, more like the old authority figure in the sky than as our own intrinsic essence. This perception of God is a variation of the projected parental authority. The ego tends to see betrayal from a very limited us-versus-them perspective, the "doer" and the "done-to."

From this place caused by early childhood wounding that cuts us off from the heart—wounding that teaches us that loss creates pain—we are quite unable to see the perfection of the awkward and painful situations. Then there is the gradual conditioning of seeing the world through the lens of good and bad, a variation of negative and positive, or of painful and pleasurable. By the time the conditioning process is finished, we have a completely subjective perception of negative and positive, judging things as good and bad, right and wrong, painful or pleasurable, eventually landing up in a very limited paradigm of awareness. From there we do not and cannot see the intrinsic perfection of all that manifests for us when we view life from a larger and more in-depth perspective.

So, as we begin to witness the parts of us that view both God and the betrayal from the egoic perspective, we can begin to forgive. Undoing this knot means forgiving the world for being the hellhole that it appears to be, forgiving God for creating the world as a hell-hole, and forgiving God for putting *us* in the hellhole of the world.

Begin this piece of work on forgiveness by holding the idea of it in your meditation, not necessarily all the time, but beginning to work with it. It has to be held deeply and looked at over and over, because there will be parts of you that think, "Why should I forgive? I want revenge, not forgiveness! I want satisfaction, not forgiveness!" Forgiveness means letting the whole thing go, and letting it be okay. And if there is a fighter in there, you will feel it.

Or the situation could go in the direction of your feeling that you have already forgiven the betrayal as much as possible and that there is nothing more to do. This is the tricky part because it can be deceptive. Since our awareness is divided between the conscious mind and unconscious mind, the forgiveness reaches down only through the conscious mind. We tend to forget that there are most likely deeper places in the unconscious where we are still holding out and resisting forgiveness. Because of this, it is necessary to keep digging deeper into the unconscious to find where the holdouts are and to bring them into alignment with forgiveness.

Sometimes that may seem like a lot to ask. So we must remember that within us is this wonderful, quiet perceiver that is eternal, whereas all the betrayals are *not* part of our eternality. They are held in the egoic consciousness that we are choosing to let go of. They are not eternal. That is unless we choose to take them with us when we die, into our next life, and again into the next.

Betrayal becomes nothing when we get down to what really matters to our eternal Self—knowing our eternality and its state of perfect love. And it is possible for us to find that place of knowing during times of meditation, contemplation, or processing. We can use that time to drop into the deeply hidden inner places to find the holdouts and to come into the forgiveness and the letting go that bring release.

BEING BUSY UNTO DEATH

It is harder, if not completely impossible, to do that when we are always caught up in worldly activity. If our life is always made up of busy-ness, distraction, and doing, and if we never make time to clear ourselves, we will be unprepared for death. When our time comes to die, we will find ourselves contemplating and taking stock of the meaning of life. It is then that we will ask ourselves what really counted in life, what *mattered*. Then it becomes very obvious that what mattered were all the times that we held to love—believed in it, gave it, and sought to become it. It is all too clear then that betrayal, resentment, revenge, and hatred have no value and do not matter at all.

So, at the time of death, those negatives will not be the things that have any value to our soul, because those are all disconnected, transitory states. The people that we have blamed and the resentments we have held toward them are like dust—ashes. The things that matter are those that are eternal, like love. We will remember the moments when we really loved, when we really were pure and pristine with others. These moments will stay with us because they are part of our eternal essence. We will be very motivated to discard the other baggage very quickly, letting go of it in an instant, the instant we recognize it as being nothing of any consequence.

So forgiveness is the process of connecting to our eternality, to our luminosity, and to the quiet simplicity of our cleared mind. It is instrumental in bringing life into a proper perspective, allowing us to see what really matters—what is eternal and what is not, what is real and what is not, and what counts and what does not. And there is no easier place to do this kind of discernment than sitting quietly in meditation.

UNDERSTANDING BETRAYAL

When we were born, we had our universal perceiver intact. This universal perceiver is the one who knows truth. This perceiver encounters a very controlling and domineering world. There are many, many ways to be dominated. You can be dominated with cruelty *and* with kindness, which is something we do not often realize.

Most parents assume that a baby is a pretty stupid lump of flesh, although, this is not quite as prevalent today as it was a few decades ago. And so, the baby comes up against dominance and control. It may not be overt dominance from day one, but it certainly is control. The little child is told day in and day out that it does not know anything, or at least that assumption is just made. Most parents also assume that the baby must be taught everything about the world—how to think, how to see, how to perceive! The honoring of the perceiver in the baby does not happen very often. Sure, the baby has poor motor skills, but everything else is intact in a latent form. Most parents no longer have an understanding of the true perceiver in themselves since the way of this world is that the true perceiver gives over to the false perceiver.

How do you react when someone tries to dominate, manipulate, or control you? Think about it for a moment.

From early childhood, we develop a variety of reactions, and these become roles that we play—personas. If someone tries to dominate, manipulate, and control us, we begin putting up guards. The rebel is one of the personas that may develop. The victim is another. The rebel is the one who bucks authority and feels powerful, and the victim is the one who submits to authority and feels powerless.

The way that the world impacts a baby is that the baby's true perceiver is not seen, heard, understood, or validated, but it *does* get validation for its responses to everybody else's programmed blindness. If it begins to react to what it sees outside, there will be a response from the "world outside." It will connect to the baby, allowing the baby to connect to it. "Oh, look. Little Johnny's developing a personality! Isn't that cute." Sometimes this may be a negative kind of connection, but not always. Often it is positive. In the end all that matters is that the baby will feel connected. And so the coating of the personality comes into place, and the true perceiver is discounted.

Under parental authority the dualistic personas, whether the dominant, rebellious, and assertive one or the passive, submissive, victimized one, begin to be instituted in the baby. As far as the world is concerned, the baby is beginning to develop a personality.

In the course of this childhood development, the original perceiver seems to become hidden by the developing personality. This is the coating of the core by the shadow of the egoic veils. Yet the good news is that it is not completely lost. It is just disguised. Despite the fact that the life force and the awareness of eternity get clouded over, the perceiver is still there fortunately, still looking through those eyes—eyes that have become clouded by the programmed concepts around life.

So, in its pure form, unadulterated by the attributes of the developing personality, that perceiver, which we call "I," a word we use dozens of times a day, is still the universal perceiver—the Self. The small "i" is really the eternal I. Ultimately there is no difference.

The perceiver, disguised by the veil of the personality, is connected all the way to the core, the Self within you, pure non-dual consciousness. Even when the perceiver is pretending to be the personality, it looks straight out from the core place—straight out through your own eyes.

There are ways to get back into it, ways to get through the cloudiness of the worldly persona. There are doorways through the centers of each of the chakras, especially through to the center of the heart chakra, where a deeper, unified truth can be perceived—something we respond to like lungs gasping for a first breath of fresh air.

By using the seven keys to open the locks between the chakras, the chakras themselves also open to a deeper level, and we have our first taste of our universal birthright. Eventually all of the locks are open, giving us our realization of the core and our unified state. The perception of truth opens all the way through the body and can then manifest in our daily life.

NON-DUAL TRUTH —
NO ONE BETRAYED ANYONE

In a manner of speaking, we did this betrayal to ourselves—we caused it to happen. We are nobody's victim here, even though it may appear that way. How can we explain this? *Our* souls chose those parents, who were actually impeccable enough to institute the blueprint that *we* designed at a soul level as the program for life in the personality. We chose our parents because they could give us what we needed—not necessarily what we wanted, but what we needed.

The ultimate betrayal was to ourselves. If we can find it inside us to forgive ourselves for choosing to come to this world, for choosing apparently to give up our true Self, the other betrayals almost seem irrelevant. As the Vedantists say, "If you know who you are, nothing else matters." In our unconscious we spin around in heartbreak, assuming that we have lost our true self, because we do not know who we are, or we think we do not know who we are. But we do.

If some part of you holds onto anger and blame, feeling like a victim, and you perceive that something was done to you, this is not a clear understanding of how things work. [*There is no one doing anything to anyone*] This is the highest truth. Anything else is just an appearance. Things only appear to happen in the dream that is this phenomenal world.

There is only an appearance of you and the outside. In reality there is only one unified state—all of us. Although we seem to be functioning as separate and autonomous in this world, which means that we are independent units functioning independently of divine intelligence, that is an appearance. It is truly not so. *There really is no separation between each of us and the true Self.* Therefore, there really is no independent person doing anything to anyone. Life with its doings and happenings is all <u>the *lila,*</u> the Sanskrit word for <u>the play of consciousness.</u> It is like a magnificently choreographed play, in which everyone has a role, and one of its dramas is the drama of betrayal. We are each pretending in order to keep the show going.

Still, when a betrayal happens to us and when we are still in the system of separation, it feels very real. That is why Jesus spoke of using forgiveness to change ourselves. Not everyone is able to see the highest truth all the time—the truth that *no one is doing anything to anyone*. Since not everyone is capable of seeing this truth, most have to fall back on forgiveness.

Forgiveness takes a lot of faith, and that faith comes more easily if we are not fully buying into the system of separation. But it also has to do with the heart. Often it is an intuitive flash that tells us that *not* forgiving, but holding vengeful, hateful thoughts, is actually more damaging to our own system. This poison of hate and resentment will also affect the person we are projecting those thoughts onto, but in the end it is going to hurt us more. So forgiveness is the willingness to let go—of our self-importance, our pride, our hurt, our resentment, and the feeling that we have to get our pound of flesh.

Deep inside of us we do know the truth, that we are not separate and that we are love. When we awaken to the truth about our real Self and thus to love, we do not proudly and self-importantly pamper and cherish ourselves. We love ourselves in a much more respectful way, all the while knowing that our and others' baggage does not matter. It does not have to be important. That is true nobility of soul. As Shakespeare said, "To err is human and to forgive is divine." Learning to forgive is the very real awakening of our divine nature.

Yes, it is necessary initially to forgive ourselves for letting go of our perceiver and for being in the illusion of separation. Yet the highest truth is this: We as the Self did not really betray ourselves, because there never was a betrayal. How is this possible? From a non-dual point of view, if there is no subject-object split between us and the Self, then we are both the betrayer and betrayed. If we are both of those, can there really be a betrayal then? The realization that there was no betrayal begins to dawn as we go through the stages of integration of the old personality and as a non-dual *knowing* returns.

Sometimes in peak spiritual experiences we can just jump right into the non-dual understanding that *no one is doing anything to anyone.* The mind just pops open, and the truth is readily available. When these experiences happen, immediately write down this new "knowing," because shortly after, your logical mind will come in and say, "How is this possible?" All the egoic baggage that has not been cleared yet will start negating what you saw, and you will doubt yourself with thoughts such as: "What do you mean I shouldn't be exacting revenge? How can you say nothing ever happened? Look at the bruises on my body!"

Trying to see a higher truth from a lower point of view is a problem. It puts us in a double bind, which is this: If we can only see the higher truth after the locks in the body open up, but if we can't open up the locks without seeing the truth, then how do we get to see the truth?

Forgiveness becomes a jump into that higher level of awareness not usually perceptible to the third-dimensional personality. When we take that step and when the energy-flows open up in the body, we are able to directly perceive the truth that there is no betrayal. Even if parts of you are still not seeing it but are resisting and fighting it, try to let the truth in at an intellectual level. It is a first step.

If you have an axe to grind about something, and if there is still a lot of supercharged emotional energy on the issue, it is not going to give up easily. But it will if you can see even for ten seconds what the truth is. Even a brief glimpse of truth greatly weakens that charge.

BEYOND BETRAYAL, FORGIVENESS

Forgiveness is a very amazing energy field, which you will see as you begin to use this key. It is a profound letting go, expansion, and embracing of peace in the heart. Another word for forgiveness is reconciliation. It implies the harmonious coming together of previously disparate and conflicting forces. Thus forgiveness or reconciliation is the ascended state that is kindled in the heart chakra when we reconcile the polarity of betrayal and trust in the third chakra.

When we take on and stubbornly hold a polarized

position associated with power issues in the third chakra, the knot at the diaphragm develops and becomes stronger, and when we reconcile these polarities and forgive them, the knot on the diaphragm opens up, allowing our awareness to ascend into the heart. Forgiveness releases the idea of betrayal held in the mind, and the contraction betrayal creates in the physical body leaves. It also releases the associated emotional content.

The scar tissue in the emotional body is the grievance—the holding onto the idea that something bad was done to us. There must be a choice to let that go. You might say, "Okay, well so what? Somebody did something bad to me. What do *I* want to do with that?" A decision must be made. Are you going to take responsibility for it or put the responsibility for it on to someone else?

If somebody did something, which you interpreted as being bad for you, you could take responsibility for causing it. You make the choice to let it wound you and to hold it as a scar in your being, or you could just as easily choose to dump it. That is forgiveness, where you wipe the slate clean. You will feel it as a letting go and as a releasing in the diaphragm area.

So forgiveness is the mystical union of two opposing energy forces. It allows them to dissolve, and then they naturally come together, unify, and ascend into the heart.

Forgiveness, to be real and helpful, has to happen on every level. It is important to let go of the way in which we have told ourselves the story. We created the story, and we can heal it and let it go. Letting go of the grievance in the mind and letting go of the old story are the ways to start. The release in the body will follow. We can just decide we do not need them anymore, that they are meaningless to us. To release them in the body, we can meditate on the place in the body where the hard knot is held and put light and love into that spot. We are not the victims of circumstance. We are the creators, too. But until we accept that, we are powerless in the face of dominance from the outside that wounds us.

Try to accept that you are the victim *and* the dominator, that you are the betrayer *and* the betrayed—both sides. As the soul designer of all experiences, you are in fact both sides of the story. It takes an incredible generosity of spirit to do this. That is why it is a spiritual state to forgive.

While forgiveness is a state of generosity, of letting bygones be bygones, it is also a state of humility, too. You might practice saying, "Maybe there is another way to look at this, maybe this situation isn't what it appears to be." This would be really close to the truth, because nothing in this world is as it appears to be. You can also practice saying, "Maybe I brought this on myself somehow." These are ways that you can get past your wounding and victimhood while still being in the system of duality, while still being in a state of feeling separate. I believe that is what the teaching of forgiveness is about. It is not necessarily about seeing the non-dual truth, which releases you instantly when you get it. It is about being in the duality and finding ways to heal yourself.

A PROCESS

Use the polarity processing technique to help clear the egoic knot of betrayal. Find a place inside yourself where you hold a grudge. For example, against someone who wronged you in some way or against God for the unfairness of life. Write about the betrayal in your journal. Be sure to include all your feelings about it. Go back through the story and circle all the descriptive words and phrases—adjectives, adverbs, anything with a charge to it. Make a list of all those words and phrases down the left-hand column of a page. Then in the right-hand column, write the opposites. Remember that these are the polarities that comprise the ego, that lock us into attractions and repulsions and that keep us stuck in the limitation and the duality of the separate system. Make an offering of the list and give it all back to spirit. Let it all go, knowing none of it is who you truly are. You are eternity. In a meditation, release it, forgive the betrayal, and try to feel the movement of energy into the heart.

A Prayer

Oh Eternity, please take all of these states of mind which are unbalanced, and balance and clear them. Do this so that I may see more clearly and find my way home more easily. I offer up these feelings of betrayal, and I ask to be able to forgive and to live more in my heart. I give thanks, knowing it will be done.

A Meditation

Please meditate for a few minutes and work with that original betrayal inside your body. Imagine along the midline of your body, the core, that you have a column of light made of the white light of eternity—what we know in the physical universe as star energy. It is the same light as the stars. The veils are not dense and impenetrable. If you go inside yourself and radiate that light, it comes right through the veils. It is the light of God. Everyone has it. It is your core, and it is the core of the universe. As you do this, remember: Who needs attachment to anything when you are a star burning brightly inside the physical body? Forgive all betrayals.

THE
THIRD KEY

Not My
Will but
Thine

The awakening of the throat chakra is the dawning of our creativity. As we begin to use creativity, we must feel and use the force of will as part of the act of creation. Wanting to be a successful creator or manifester motivates us to where we must begin to access the power of the universal mind—the source of creative power. Thus we must begin to open up to the greater Self in our efforts to reach the heights of that ability to create. In opening up we are actually becoming co-creators with the universal mind. Often this union becomes a completely conscious activity. This level of becoming an artist of life is the beginning of an ascension.

There is a much deeper level of awakening that involves bringing the kundalini, the energy of ascension, all the way up to the throat. When we use this key here it produces the effect of awakening in us a clear awareness of existing beyond the personal. We can feel a sense of our fellowship with humanity, and our creativity is directed toward increasing this goodwill for all. We are beginning to merge with the Divine. While it is in the heart chakra that we first feel the presence of the Divine, it is upon opening this lock into the throat chakra that the heart energy begins to connect with the universal mind. We find we wish to serve more—both the Divine and humanity.

The key for the lock between the heart chakra and the throat chakra, "Not my will, but Thine," relates to our use of will—our own autonomous will—and also how our will interconnects with the divine will. "Not my will but Thine" were the words that Jesus is reputed to have spoken when he prayed in the Garden of Gethsemane the night before the crucifixion. He was in the garden praying for guidance and information, and he received the divine communication that he was to surrender to the events that were about to occur. This was his response, his way of verbalizing his surrender to divine will.

WILL
What then is will? And what does it mean to have an autonomous will separated from the divine will?

Will is "supercharged attention," a force that is focused and directed toward some purpose. Let's take a look at what I mean by supercharged attention. This is a very powerful and mysterious force. It is the presence of universal mind. Universal mind is the most powerful force that exists. In fact it is the only force that truly exists. All other powers and forces are manifestations of this presence of universal mind, or what we call "will."

Why describe it as supercharged? It is supercharged because it is undivided, and undivided attention has the most power. When we talk about undivided attention, we usually mean that its focus in us is not distracted by anything else. But when we talk about it being undivided in a more universal context, this means that it is non-dual—not divided into two. This means its power is not diluted as a result of being divided into negative and positive polarity. Its power would be halved by the duality, undermined particularly by the negative side of the duality.

So what we see here is that the power of will associated with universal mind lies in its non-dual state. In the higher dimensions where the frequencies vibrate at high speed, there is almost no duality. Thus the more unified the attention, the faster the vibration and the more powerful an effect the focus of attention has. It is supercharged by its one-pointedness, or single-mindedness.

Attention is something we all have. It is the way we focus our own energy and awareness into intention and motivation. To us, in our separate and autonomous state, it is the strength we find we have, the inner force or inner power that we use to control the circumstances of our lives, either to manifest our desires or to curtail them.

From the perspective of our limited state, attention or will seems to be innately built into our mind and our awareness. It manifests in life as focus, determination, perseverance, and the ability to transcend adversity. It is the power we have to hold everything in our lives together in the way we desire. When it manifests in our "separate" awareness, we feel it to be our own innate ability to make things happen.

Yet as we explore the true nature of will, it is obvious that will as described above belongs to universal mind, as its own force, and that the power we feel as our own is in fact being "loaned" to us by the presence of the universal mind. What we call "our attention" is really a manifestation of divine, universal attention.

How then is our will different from divine will? As we discussed earlier, in essence it is not. The energetic power of separate will is, in fact, the presence of divine will acting in and through us. The difference lies in our perspective of what God is.

From our perspective while in a state of separation and autonomy from the whole, we feel that this presence of will that is in us is ours. We do not recognize where it comes from because we hold an underlying belief in our egoic mind about our separation from God. At root we hold the belief that we are at the very least somewhat separate from God. This belief has a lot to do with the way we have been taught to see that which we call God.

In our third-dimensional unconscious is a perception that God is a being in whose image we were made, who is outside of us and thus separate from us. We do not see that we are energetically connected to God. We also do not see that in creation there is only one energy presence, out-picturing in the many vibratory tones of creation, and that everything is completely interconnected within this one energy presence, throughout all of existence. We do not see this because while we live in a third-dimensional ego, we are experiencing an inner programming that tells us we are separate from everything else. We are given an autonomous will—something we call free will—ours to do what we want with. However, as our will is used to fulfill our plan for our life, it often comes into conflict with the plan held by the divine will. Then there is a thwarting of our plan and the squashing of our willful hopes and dreams by supposedly outside and unforeseen circumstances.

Although we receive the force of divine will through us, because our awareness exists in duality, this force of attention is not usually non-dual—although once in a while it can be, when we are really single-minded. Rather, it is most often held in duality, and thus its power is greatly weakened, cut in half by the hidden and usually negative side of our dualistic state—something we perceive to be an outside force opposing our desires. None the less it remains the same force that holds the cosmos in place, however adulterated.

The non-dual force of attention that is universal mind passes through us disguised as our own will. It becomes distorted by the state of duality in which we live here in this world. It polarizes and loses most of its power because of the hidden side of the polarity. This loss of power as a result of duality makes us experience what we call failure of our plan and is one of the ways we are ultimately drawn to surrender to divine will.

SURRENDERING

There are other ways in which our will becomes distorted. We tend to run this universal will through our patterns of worldly desire. Desires that are held in our small, egoic mind are usually not desires that serve the soul's overall purpose of our lives. Supercharged attention, as much as we are able to access it, is a force that we need to use impeccably, which means to use it in alignment with our soul's overall purpose. Most humans, feeling that they are in charge of their own lives, are not aware of their soul's larger purpose and tend to fall into choices that are mostly small and self-serving. They attempt to use the force of will often in trivial and distracting pursuits to satisfy the temptations and concepts of the limited mind. This greatly reduces their power of will. There is an innate guilt that goes with being autonomous and pleasing one's limited self, and that guilt dilutes the force of will.

It is using this force of will to get the things that we think we need but that have very little value to the soul's purpose that is the use and abuse of the power of will. In other words, the will can perform within the human egoic pattern as a source of personal power for the limited ego's purpose, or it can be used in service to the soul's highest aspirations on its journey toward the clear light of cosmic wisdom.

As we look at this third key, we see that surrender of the old ways of using will is an important and meaningful aspect of ascending toward reunion with our Self. This brings the separate will into alignment with divine will.

Surrender, in spiritual terms, is the surrender of the separate ego—that part of us that believes itself to be separate from the Divine. The belief in our separate, autonomous identity is part and parcel of living in the third dimension. In this dimension our free will is our God-given right. It is our free will and freedom of choice that we have in this world which also allow us to be as selfish and as trivial as we please. There is no right and wrong in this. It is not a judgment, but is simply an individual choice, and in the third dimension everyone has the right of choice.

Yet if we wish to ascend, we must look long and hard at what this freedom of choice and what our free will really mean. A first glance reveals that in view of the truth of non-separation between us and the universal mind, we begin to see that our autonomy is just an idea held in the limited mind. It does not really exist. Or rather, we are not surrendering anything except the *idea* of our free will—since there is no such thing as the separate state. The separate state with its separate will is part of the appearance in the phenomenal world. In truth there cannot be any "my will."

Then how does our free will manifest? It is a trick, sleight of hand made to appear as though we are actually autonomous and as though the will is ours, when in fact we are really borrowing the divine will and running it through the third-dimensional programming. This is the program of free will, given as part of the design, the blueprint of the third dimension.

Thus what we are actually surrendering is the program of our separate, autonomous state—the deluded ideas of separation and of separate will. As we do that, we surrender our right to play at being like God by being in charge. And we give up this deluded idea in favor of actually becoming conscious of our original oneness with the divine will.

Yet as we do the releasing, even if we now understand that we are not the ego, we must speak from and for the ego in order to dissolve the program. Thus we say, "Not my will but thine."

Using this key for the throat chakra, we begin realizing that we are not limited individuals, living selfish lives, with only our own well-being to think of. We become more available to our larger self and over time let go of any heavily personalized focus. We must allow a growth toward seeing our fellowship with others and becoming more universal in vision and approach to life.

A PROCESS

The process of using this key starts as a mental idea, where you say to spirit, "Yes, I am willing to let go of that." The choice to let go of your free will at any given moment is also the choice to give up separation. And it is also the choice to realize that there really is no such thing as free will, that it is bound up in the erroneous notion that we are separate, autonomous beings. However, as you look at making this choice, your ego will feel a sense of loss of its freedom and perhaps balk at the idea.

The following exercise is called "the square technique" and is explained more thoroughly in *The Marriage of Spirit—Enlightened Living in Today's World*. This particular square will help you to release any unconscious egoic aspects that prevent you from accessing divine will. Write a list of all the thoughts and emotions that come to mind under each of these four headings:

Why you desire to have free will

Why you fear having free will

Why you desire to give up free will

Why you fear giving up free will

When you are complete, let the whole thing go. Make an offering to spirit of the lists and ask to be free of all egoic limitations and imbalances in your use of will.

A PRAYER

Oh Eternity, I offer up my egoic desires and fears of having free will and of surrendering my free will. Please bring me into balance and show me the true meaning of Jesus' words, "Not my will but thine."

A MEDITATION

Sit comfortably and take several deep, full, relaxing breaths. Now take another deep breath, filling up your lungs completely. With your lungs full and expanded, gently but firmly push down on your diaphragm area. Then exhale completely, feeling that area soften and release. Try this one or two more times to relax the body and the breath fully. Now visualize and focus your attention on the subtle core of light running down the midline of the body, allowing your attention to gently reside in that effulgence. After a few moments, invite your consciousness to become relaxed and passive. Let go and surrender to experience the presence of divine will. Allow that presence to be the container that holds your consciousness. Continue to meditate until you sense that you are finished. Use this as an opportunity to let divine will dictate both the experience and the duration of the meditation.

THE
FOURTH KEY

HAVE FAITH
IN THE
SUPPORT OF
THE INVISIBLE
REALMS

HAVING FAITH IN THE SUPPORT OF THE INVISIBLE REALMS IS THE KEY FOR THE LOCK BETWEEN THE ROOT CHAKRA AND THE SECOND CHAKRA. The invisible realms have always been present with us and always will be. They are inseparable from this and every other realm. All of creation is one perfect whole. Because we have become locked into a narrow vibratory bandwidth, we have lost sight of them. By rekindling our faith in their existence, we begin to open up the old inter-dimensional doorways that once upon a time were open to us. We are consciousness, and as consciousness we exist simultaneously on all vibratory bandwidths. The part of our awareness limited to this realm is programmed for that limitation. Actually we are everywhere. We can and do function consciously or unconsciously in all the different bandwidths.

This key is about unlocking the fear that we experience around the issue of our survival and the way we use egoic control to survive. It addresses, as do all the keys one way or another, the dissolution of the apparent separation between the human and the Divine—"me" as subject and "God" as object. This apparent separation also creates a subject-object relationship between ourselves and the world. As we saw in the previous key, "Not my will but Thine," this subject-object relationship complicates our lives enormously, even while giving us the experience of autonomy.

As we look at the situation historically, we see that the era of the root chakra was the era of the hunter-gatherer. This was a time when humans were reliant on their instincts to guide them to food sources. What is instinct? This faculty is the rather primitive use of intuition. Instinct and intuition are a direct connection to universal presence and intelligence—that flow of all-knowingness—although in the case of instinct there is not the self-awareness to know that. Beings such as animals still use instinct to guide them through their lives, especially in the instance of wild animals to their food sources. They are directly plugged into universal knowledge, which includes knowing where food is to be found when they need it. Of course the opposite would also be true. They would have to accept being in the wrong place at the wrong time, a place where there was no food, which would mean having to face starvation. Animals are very accepting of their fate in this way, as was early humankind—the hunter-gatherer.

In time, the gatherers, who were the women of the clans and who gathered wild grasses amongst other things, began to see that they could control the food source. By planting and tending wild grasses, they were able to store grain and could control whether or not the clan starved in the lean times. Humans were no longer obliged to live and die at the mercy of the forces of nature. This was a giant step forward in our evolution. We began trying to take control over our own lives and deaths.

This change ushered in an era where consciousness was centered in the second chakra, and the people became very involved with fertility as they tried to control the forces of nature. In their attempt to control their survival, they were no longer as surrendered to the divine will as to whether they lived or died.

As they became increasingly disconnected from higher consciousness and from a more universal sense of awareness, they began to experience greater separation and complexity in their relationship to nature. The subject-object relationship was explored in the practice of rituals and fertility rites in which they hoped to appease the forces that they perceived were controlling their fate—forces with which they were no longer aligned and which now appeared to be outside and separate from them. These forces, such as the weather, had an effect on their crops and thus a life-and-death effect on their survival.

This was the beginning of a kind of primitive religion, a way to bridge the disconnection from universal knowing and ultimately from truth. By using this key, we will undo this lock and dissolve this ancient veil by opening up, once again, our direct connection to those invisible realms.

OUR CHOICE FOR AUTONOMY

By taking matters into our own hands and taking "control" of our destiny, we were trying to control our life and death. In this we were establishing our autonomous state. And in needing to take charge and think for ourselves, we were taking our free will. In doing this we appeared to be creating a disconnection from the divine will—in a sense competing with it. Overall and over time the result was the loss of our faith—faith in the support of the invisible realms and an increasing sense of our individuality.

Opening this lock means that at a moment when we feel least filled with faith, we have to try to remember to trust in the support of the invisible realms. That support never leaves us; but since we, humanity, took our free will, our ideas of what we want and need have come into conflict with the divine intention and plan for our lives. Yet the support given by the universal mind for the evolution of our lives is always present as that universal, all-knowing presence. It is always available to us, especially when we choose to return to the original state of Oneness and connectedness, and even as we begin to seek it from our place of disconnection. It simply waits for us to wise up and to want to reconnect again.

In our fear of death and in our desire to escape it, we formed ideas about how we could control our circumstances, and we have been doing that ever since. Choosing autonomy, developing concepts about controlling our circumstances and discovering ways to make that happen have formed what we now experience as our separate mind—mind stuff that is now apparently disconnected from the universal mind.

This is the allegory of Eve and Adam choosing to defy God and eat the apple. As a result, they were driven out of the Garden of Eden, had to fend for themselves, and become autonomous. Eden was that connected state where all our needs were met. Yet all of the ideas we have about being unsupported are ultimately only ideas. If you believe the ideas held in the lower mind, then you will actually manifest the experience. Thus you will feel unsupported and alone.

FEAR OF DEATH

We fear death because we do not understand it. Viewed from the separate state, it seems like annihilation because we are unable to see if there is any continuation of our awareness beyond that moment. We hold the state of uncertainty around the death experience because of our disconnection from the invisible realms and because of our loss of faith that our lives are actually supported from that invisible presence—the universal mind, the unfathomable intelligence of existence. Because we began the journey of trying to control our circumstances, we now find it very difficult to let go of everything we have ever known, to enter the eye of the needle naked and flow freely into the unknown.

Yet we chose the state of separation, and ironically we chose it because we wanted the power that control of our circumstances gives us. But we did not realize that this would mean a disconnection from the invisible realms. As the disconnection manifested, we began to experience loss, and as we moved deeper into the polarity of separation, we actually began to experience an increase in our fear of death, which is what we had sought to escape in the first place.

To this day we work diligently at controlling our circumstances in order to stay safe and to prevent our suffering and death. We are successful in many ways, although death always wins in the end. Becoming separate has left us not only with a fear of the unknown, but also with the disconnection from directly knowing that we are supported by the invisible realms.

INSIDE AND OUTSIDE

Our lack of ability to perceive truth in the separate system means that we lack the ability to see how our outer
and inner realities are mirror reflections of each other.
The inner and the outer are actually a continuous, congruent reflection of each other. There was a time way
back in our early development when we actually lived in a
state of awareness in which the inner and outer realities
were very much one thing. This allowed us to know that
our inner consciousness affected the outside. Our attempt
to take control of our destiny initiated the separation of
the inner and the outer.

Over time humans developed ever-increasing degrees of separation between the outer and inner realities.
The separation was based on the choice to take care of
ourselves by taking control of our circumstances. There
was a choice to play God—to be "as gods" with domin-
ion over the earth instead of being part of the great
wholeness of universal presence. We gradually lost the
ability to see the web of life as one inter-connected
whole. This gradual loss of awareness has limited our
perception and has isolated us.

More recently in our modern era, the sense of
extreme separateness developed in classical Greece. It
was there that philosophers postulated that space was
empty. They proposed that solid objects existed in empty
space, unaffected by each other, and their invention of

"logic" birthed the rational mind. After 25 centuries of being taught this philosophy, we see the world through its lens.

Today we feel that the inside of our mind is private and completely disconnected, on the subtle energetic level, from the world around us. Not only that, but the inner, subtle dimensions of consciousness are also missing from our perception. Our inability to trust in and to perceive the invisible realms has locked us into a very limited bandwidth of perception. Most importantly, we have lost the ability to discern cause and effect, and to see how the mind directly causes the actions that lead to most of the effects that we see outside of us.

The point here is that our perception of inner seeing being separate from outer seeing is a mental construct that we have created. We do not remember how this perception came into being, therefore we accept it as reality. This fact is certainly worth pondering—that our sense of objective and subjective reality is a man-made construct that developed over time. In case this does not sound plausible to you, think of all the many stories of how children see fairies, angels, or other beings that the adults cannot see and thus repudiate. If the adults disparage the child's seeing, the child, who wants the adults' approval, will lose this inner sight.

As you begin to awaken once again to the existence of the subtle realms that over time have become invisible to you, you are becoming capable of opening the doors of perception, of seeing that you also exist on those other levels and of drawing your power from that source.

A Process

Do a square on death and survival. Make four lists:

The desire for death
The fear of death
The desire for survival
The fear of survival

When you are complete, make an offering to spirit of the lists. Let it all go. Ask to be free of all egoic attraction and repulsion around death and survival. Offer your gratitude for the support from the grace of the invisible realms.

A Prayer

Oh Eternity, I offer up these lists and give back to source all my desires and fears of death and survival. Please free me from all egoic attachment to them. Please free me from doubt that I am perfectly supported at all times by the invisible realms. Please strengthen my faith in the support of the invisible realms.

A MEDITATION

Sit comfortably and take several deep, relaxing, letting-go breaths. Use the expanded lungs to gently and firmly push down and relax the diaphragm area. Try this several more times to relax the body and awareness completely. Make sure that your spine is upright, without straining. Think of gently resting on your bones, visualizing a nicely stacked, straight spine. Now visualize the core as a luminous, fluorescent tube running down the center of your subtle body, slightly in front of your spine. By visualizing it, you begin to feel its presence. Sit with your attention on the core, and allow yourself to become very still and centered. Once you feel comfortable with this, allow your attention to migrate downward, toward the lower chakras. Open your awareness to and feel the vibratory quality of the energies of the lower chakras. See if you can feel the fear of death and the desire for survival down there. Then gently bring that energy upward through the core. Finally pull it through the heart chakra and release it upward, giving it back to source. By meeting and releasing your fear and survival issues like this in meditation, as a vibration, they begin to lose their hold on your awareness. Make this downward sweep several times during the meditation, working within the light and stillness of the core, feeling the support and love of that luminosity.

VIEW
THE EGO
IMPERSONALLY

THIS KEY OPENS THE LOCK SEPARATING THE SEC-
OND CHAKRA FROM THE THIRD CHAKRA, and it is
an invitation to begin seeing your egoic self in a
detached way, with impersonal eyes—to begin witnessing it from your larger Self. We are all more than capable of witnessing the ego from outside of its patterning,
since we are not the ego.

We saw in the previous chapter how gradually, over
the course of history, humanity was learning to use the
power of will. As we moved into the third chakra era, we
began to revere this power. By glorifying it as the ability
to use greater control, the power of will became synony-
mous with the individual self. Humankind was learning
to *own* the power—as though it belonged exclusively
within the human form and mind.

As the collective consciousness of humanity developed to the point of being ready to ascend out of the second chakra era, the desire to control life's circumstances became more and more entrenched. The autonomous self, the one who wants to be in charge of and to care for itself, developed in new and unusual ways.

The human choice to be autonomous grew into a denial of innate, instinctive connectedness, a quality held by all the other life forms on earth. Humanity was becoming increasingly disconnected from the deep inner knowing of truth. As human brainpower increased, the separate mind developed the ability to "think for itself," and a separate self, with a separate will, very dedicated to its own individuality began to emerge. This new identity was defined by and bound up in the power that individuals were able to hold on their own. There was little or no recognition of power, or will, as coming from universal presence. The power had been completely usurped by the individual, and God was now seen as outside of the individual.

In our modern era we have taken this to an extreme. Thus the sense of "being the ego" and of living in disconnection and separation from the interconnected web of life has been cemented firmly into place—to the point that it is now the defining characteristic of the third chakra consciousness and the third dimension. Humanity perceives itself well and truly cut off from source. We developed religion in the attempt to reinstate the connection. But prayer and ritual were being offered to a God or gods outside of the human mind and located somewhere else, in a place called Heaven.

As we view the ego impersonally, we are able to see that we are not separate from a God outside of us, and we are able to experience our connectedness to source, loosening the knot that restricts the flow of kundalini between the second and third chakras. Using this key, we begin to reverse this ancient growth toward the glory of the individual self to the exclusion of all else. We can look at how our issues are held in the patterns that have formed from the programming we have received—patterns that are typical during this era and inherited from the many preceding generations.

Worthy of note is the understanding that we do not lose our unique individuality as we complete our understanding of and graduate from the third dimension, when awareness finally enters the heart chakra. Rather, we move into a paradigm known as "unity in diversity." While retaining our unique individuality, we no longer see ourselves as so special that we feel entitled to exclude all else—having little respect for other species and the rest of creation. Anne Rich

POWER AND POWERLESSNESS

Power and powerlessness is the over-arching duality governing the third-chakra consciousness. As we moved into the third-chakra era, we wanted the power. We took it, and we have evolved a whole system that revolves around power and its opposite, powerlessness.

As described in chapter four about will, we are constrained in the use of our power by the nature of duality. Duality is the handicap, the limitation we must face in this game of power. Duality has given us powerlessness as an opposite to this thing to which we are so addicted, forcing us to contend with its shadow nature.

As we saw in chapter one, duality spins the pairs of opposites so that they move in and out of our conscious awareness. The spinning of all the pairs of opposites is governed by the laws of duality—one of which is the law of attraction and repulsion. Because of the law of attraction and repulsion, we are subject to another law of duality, which is that everything in time will turn into its opposite. So for example, when we are attracted to something like power, we must also deal with its opposite—powerlessness.

In the third dimension duality is extremely polarized. Its spin has become a rather hazardous dance, the dance of our aspiration to be like God and to play as gods. It is here that we dance between our concepts of Heaven and Hell, not always sure which is which. And when we win some power, feeling like the gods we believe ourselves to be, duality spins again, and we lose it all. We fall and feel utterly shamed and humiliated, as though we had been cast down from Heaven into Hell. We feel completely unworthy. As we fall, we mistakenly perceive that something stronger and more powerful than us "out there" caused our fall, and to it we have ascribed omnipotent power. This is God the omnipotent, more powerful than we, and furthermore, capable of being angry with us. How else could we have fallen?

This is the story of the third dimension. What we do not see is that the spin of duality casts us down and that because of it we are only gods some of the time. Our challenge now is that we must face this reality that we have created and have chosen to enter and learn the lessons it has to teach. We must learn to navigate this roller coaster, since that is the game of the third dimension.

UNDERDOG AND OVERDOG

As we try to hold on to the power we sought and won, we begin to complicate our minds and our lives. The original simplicity of our earlier state is now lost, and our separate mind has become one of great complexity and convolution. We have learned deviousness through attempting to control power. We have learned to manipulate, dominate, and betray in a vain attempt to stay on top.

Since everyone is cycling through power and powerlessness, we envy and covet the power that someone else has when we are in a down-and-out phase. We are capable of trying to grab power from the one who has it in the moment, as though power was a commodity. We ascribe power to material things and have gone to war either to get more of them or to hold on to those we already have.

AS YOU SOW, SO SHALL YOU REAP

In our modern era we seem to have completely forgotten that in our separate state we are subject to the law of cause and effect. Even though most people would say that they know about cause and effect, few people actually practice living their lives with that understanding moderating their actions. When we abuse power, we pay a karmic price for our actions. In fact the old adage "an eye for an eye and a tooth for a tooth" is really a rather primitive description of the laws of karma. Yet strangely it has been misunderstood so that it now means that we are entitled to enact retribution on others for the things they have done to us. Since we do not believe in divine justice, which the law of cause and effect reflects, we once again need to take matters into our own hands and to make sure that justice is done.

THE GENDER BIAS

Any discussion about the third chakra power consciousness must address the disparity of power between men and women, for it is here that the gender gap is at its most extreme. While the genders may simply be aspects of the two sides of the androgynous soul consciousness, it is only in the third dimension that masculine/yang and feminine/yin energies materialize into a huge gender bias between men and women. Dominance, or power over others, is the most significant feature of the third dimension. Its most common manifestation is the way it has gradually been structured so that men function from a superior position to wield power over women. While there are healthy signs of change now in the Western world, overall there is no sign yet of significant global movement toward real equality here. Equality is not likely to manifest in the third dimension. It is the state we will see manifesting when we choose to move into the fourth dimension.

In third-dimensional consciousness, the polarities of better–worse and superior–inferior are defined in all areas of life: race, religion, nationality, skin color, sexual orientation, financial abundance, education, class, and so forth. This is just how we are when power is involved. We take diversity and stratify it. This is power and powerlessness.

The roles of power and powerlessness played out between men and women at the surface of life are not what they appear to be. It is our soul that plays both sides of every polarity, both the powerful and the powerless role. Below the surface is a soul drama played out between both of the gender essences contained in one soul. The characteristic of the us-and-them consciousness found in this world is that we perceive separation and do not acknowledge that we are playing both roles.

As we own that we are both sides, the dominator/perpetrator and the loser/victim, we are able to integrate all the many schisms between the masculine and feminine. Also, in the case of racism and all diverse aspects of society shrouded in prejudice, this principle of one soul playing both sides also applies.

Those that feel powerless are projecting their power outside themselves, giving it away. Women give it to their men. Victims give it to their tyrants, and the weak and passive give it to the aggressive and assertive. It is necessary for the one who feels powerless to take back his/her power, to develop his/her own inner power again. The perpetrators of this world are using the projected and abdicated power of the weak to dominate. If the weak are willing to own their power, then equality begins to grow inside them.

THE SEEMINGLY SEPARATE SELF

We are not the ego or the personality. We are much larger and are quite capable of orchestrating the experience, the drama, of a life lived in duality. We do this for the lessons involved. The lessons are designs created in consciousness so that there is a plan, a destiny to live out. Our separate self is a form that exists to play out the drama. In identifying with the personality, we are identifying with the false self, an identity that is designed specifically for the play.

The separate system demands that the drama be played out from a place of forgetfulness. So, long before we are adults, we have forgotten the true "I" and have come to believe that we are the being who has emerged from the many years of the conditioning process. We have become someone who identifies with all the qualities and attributes that are now part and parcel of the personality.

THE NEUTRAL WITNESS IS AWAKE

As we become aware that we are more than we seem to be in our personality, we begin to open to higher consciousness. We begin to develop a witness. The witness is the part of us that is outside the personality. It has the ability to observe the ego's mind stuff moment to moment. Using the witness we can begin to break the patterning that holds us in the third dimension. By observing the patterns that make us overreactive and get us caught up in dramas, we can begin to change them. By not making the patterns personal, we detach from them. So, shifting our perception to witnessing the personality is immediately possible and extraordinarily beneficial.

At first it does take a bit of reorientation to be able to see ourselves *being* the limited personality. But the fact is that we can actually witness the personality from a viewpoint *outside* the personality structure itself. This, in itself, proves that we are not exclusively locked into the personality. Nor are we the personality. Our true nature is as unlimited consciousness. As we see and understand the limiting patterns of the personality, so are we liberated from them and able to know ourselves as an eternal, loving presence. Recognition is liberation.

To begin developing and strengthening the witness, it is enough simply to ask inwardly for this to happen. In a prayer or affirmation in your journal, ask that your witness officially be instituted. This initiates the process. You can repeat the prayer or affirmation as often as you like—weekly, daily, or many times a day. This will help to strengthen the witness. The more frequently, the better. This not only consciously reminds you that you are not the personality, but you also invite the magic of grace to assist you in remembering. Over time, as a natural by-product of using the seven keys and processing, your witness will develop and grow.

THE WAY OF NEUTRALITY

The witness walks the middle way, sometimes known as the razor's edge. It is the way of neutrality, where we surrender the idea that we should be attracted or repulsed by anything, neither to the negative nor to the positive side of any polarity. We choose instead to identify with the neutral place, the center point between the two sides. Here the witness has the power of observation without the reactivity of judgment. Developing the ability to view life from the neutral position assists enormously in extricating us from the turning of the wheel of karma. The neutral place is the center, the eye of the storm, the still-point, a place of equanimity.

The neutral witness is a critical component in transformation and ascension. That neutral position is really what is also described as being centered. When someone is in the neutral witness, they are awake. The center is the core, the shushumna. Knowing this place consciously keeps us stable, balanced, and grounded. The blessing it brings is that it allows us to see the big picture and to view the ego impersonally. The witness is actually our connection to the Self.

As the witness engages in everyday experiences, it helps to clear the mental and emotional bodies and to awaken them. Having a witness wakes us up! We are actually awake when we are in it because we are out of the ego.

While in the witness we are living from the soul, a much deeper awareness than the personality. Witnessing takes us there by allowing awareness to ascend out of the old reality. It is integral to the process of ascension. It helps awareness to leave one level and to move to another. Moving consciousness to another paradigm is no small feat. To do it, everything must be done just right. With the witness anchoring the awareness in timeless eternality, it is possible to let go of the old way of being. Eventually we come to see that the witness is an opening from the limited personal mind into the universal mind.

REJECTION, BETRAYAL, AND ABANDONMENT

Rejection, betrayal, and abandonment are the emotions that the ego experiences after what we call the "fall," the apparent original disconnect and separation from source. It is our primal disconnect and is directly linked to the key for this chapter. This primal separation is echoed in infancy as we come down the birth canal. In this way it is stamped into the blueprint for this life.

When we feel rejected, it is very painful, and we take it personally. We usually feel diminished, slighted, worthless, and even betrayed. Rejection hurts the heart very deeply, while betrayal ties up the knot of Vishnu, and abandonment ends up in the stomach area as a hollow emptiness—an actual descent of consciousness. With abandonment we lose the sense of being filled up or fulfilled. This is the beginning of the deprived-child consciousness.

Many people feel rejected, betrayed, and abandoned as infants. When infants do not have their needs met, they interpret it as being abandoned. If an infant's mother feels overwhelmed or thinks for a moment that she wishes she did not have the baby, the baby could feel utterly rejected, betrayed, and abandoned. Sometimes the infant perceives abandonment in many instances when it really is not there. As a result of feeling abandoned as infants, we take it very personally and "fall" down into loss, despair, desperation, separation, and so forth, and the negative ego is born.

If we fear being rejected, then probably in early infancy we experienced being rejected and are afraid that it will happen again. If it had not happened once already, we would not have the fear of it. Somewhere deep in the recesses of our mind is the memory of a rejection that was more than we could bear, and we continue to run away from it even as adults.

How much of your life is influenced by your fear of feeling rejected? If even a little bit, it is coming from the infant that became overwhelmed and had no way to deal with it. The part of us that fears rejection is the infant that is still alive and well inside us and is running this piece of our life. That overwhelmed state is associated with past history, with the infant who had no recourse other than to isolate or suppress its pain.

The infant response to rejection, which is to try and run away from it to prevent it from ever happening again, does not work. If we are isolating out of fear of rejection, we are feeling the rejection and making it real. In that case, we might as well go out and get really rejected. It is just the same thing. This is the way we, as adults, are haunted by a past experience of rejection. It echoes throughout daily life constantly.

It is essential that we learn to deal with rejection with adult eyes, adult feelings, and adult decision-making. For true healing to take place, we must learn to parent the infant with the witness. To do this it is best to be taken back to that early infant rejection and to feel the feelings with the perspective of an adult. It is helpful to find a therapist who can help us to remember that experience, relive it, process it, and heal it. It is also helpful to practice the key, "View the ego impersonally," moment to moment as we witness the feelings of rejection when they arise. When we can see rejection with impersonal eyes, it will never have power over us again.

A PROCESS

Use the polarity-processing technique to help clear the egoic patterning of rejection. This will also help to strengthen the witness:

Write a story about an experience of rejection in your journal. It can be from the distant past or present-time. Be sure to include all your feelings about it. Don't economize with the paper. Be as thorough as you possibly can. Go back through the story and circle all the descriptive words and phrases—adjectives, adverbs, anything with a charge to it. Make a list of all those words and phrases down the left-hand column of a page. Then in the right-hand column, write the opposites. Make an offering of the list and give it all back to Spirit. Let it all go, knowing none of it is who you truly are. You are eternity. In a meditation, release it, view it all with impersonal eyes, and try to feel the movement of energy between the second and third chakras.

A Prayer

Oh Eternity, please take all of these states of mind which are unbalanced in this pattern, and balance and clear them. Do this so that I may see more clearly and find my way home more easily. I offer up the feelings of rejection, and I ask to be able to view the ego impersonally more and more. Please institute my witness and help it to grow stronger moment by moment. I give thanks knowing it will be done.

A Meditation

Our commitment to equality will help facilitate movement from the third chakra to the fourth. In your meditation, contemplate the idea of equality. Begin with deep, relaxing breaths, expanding the lungs and gently pushing down on the diaphragm to really release the tension in that area below the heart chakra. Allow your attention to be absorbed into the luminous core of energy within.

Now very gently bring your awareness to the heart chakra—in the center of your chest, the center of your energetic body. As you contemplate equality, feel the heart chakra as the center of balance, equality, and love. Gently keep your attention on the heart chakra in order to feel those qualities permeating throughout your being. You may experience the heart opening, almost like the petals of a rose, one after another after another. Or you may feel as if your chest is expanding and opening beyond any limitation. Or you may have a quiet, steady sense of even-ness. Simply be with the heart energy and allow your meditation to flow as it will. You can end by asking spirit to institute permanently the balanced states of equality and universal love in your awareness. Make a commitment to living them more completely.

THE
SIXTH KEY

ACCEPT
YOUR
DEATH

THIS SIXTH KEY HAS TO DO WITH FACING AND
COMING INTO EQUANIMITY WITH THE IDEA OF
DEATH. Using this key opens the root chakra
and relaxes the body, allowing the kundalini energy to
begin moving easily upward on its journey toward the
crown. The lock at the root chakra has to do with the
fear of death.

Initially, when we begin using this key, we may not
actually realize that we are holding the fear of death, yet
the idea of death is really the basis for all of our fears,
however small. If you find yourself doubting this, name
any one of your fears, and then extrapolate it to its worst-
case scenario. You will find that it involves some sort of
death—not necessarily the death of the body, but for
example, the death of a relationship, a lifestyle, a career,

or the ego. When we talk of death, we think of the experience of losing the body; however, the root chakra is associated with survival, and that means survival of all the things that we cherish and hold onto.

DETACHMENT

Learning to accept death is one way of talking about the yogic process of detachment. Detachment means the willingness to give up the practice of holding onto things and becoming much more accepting of life moving through you as a flow of change. Ultimately it is only the ego that can die.

Unless one is awake, the death of the ego means the death of the body as well, since they are so bound up together. Ascending means letting go of bodily attachment. Thus the ego can die or dissolve, and the body can remain alive. Dropping the body when one is fully awake is something different then—a conscious choice to leave.

The ego is the repository for all the ideas about life, death, what matters to us, and who we think we are. Death, in fact, is just another concept held in the mind. Life, too, is a concept held in the mind. "Oh," you might say, "but life and death are real. It's what happens every day. I've seen it with my own eyes." Yes, it does appear before our dual, physical eyes as something real, yet since we are not the egoic personality, but an expression of divine intelligence and spiritual energy, we are eternal, as spirit is eternal. We endure way beyond the parameters of this world appearance and of this bodily incarnation. We will always be and will always endure. It is the belief in the mind that tells us that death is the end. From the limited perspective of the egoic worldview, that is all that we seem to be capable of seeing. Therefore death becomes a doorway into the unknown, and the ego is programmed to fear the formlessness of the unknown.

With ascension we move through the veils, exploring the journey toward the dissolution of the ego—a journey that in many ways resembles what will happen to us when we drop the body. In fact the journey of ascension is a preparation, a training for dropping the body. It dissolves our fears around entering the formless unknown.

With the awakening of conscious knowledge of the subtle body, the journey toward realization of our eternality begins. As the kundalini makes its journey through the dimensional doorways in the subtle body and as our consciousness ascends toward knowledge of the Self at the crown, we see for ourselves beyond the shadow of any egoic doubt that we are infinite, eternal presence. The idea of death falls away as just a concept held in a limited mind.

The idea of life is the polar opposite to the idea of death, and it, too, falls into perspective as we see its limited parameters. The concept of life begins when the ego knows of its existence not too long after birth—after a period of forgetfulness—and ends in an unknown (another concept in the mind) as the body drops away. This short-term experience of self-awareness, held within the boundaries of four-score years and ten, is the egoic idea of "our life."

With the awakening of the crown chakra and re-connecting to higher consciousness, the one universal mind, we come to realize that these two moments that define a life—birth and death—are simply transitions from one phase of being to another. As we develop an ever-deepening faith in the presence of those invisible realms and of the everlasting existence that we each have as the Self, we become much more relaxed and able to let go of our fear of death.

Fear has a way of defining and dominating human life. It creates contraction in the awareness and leads to a defensive shutting down toward life. If life were lived without the fear of death shadowing it, it would be a very different experience. The fears embedded in life present us with some of our main challenges. As we make our peace with death and develop a deep under-standing of the nature of the mind and of death itself, we come into a place of equanimity and balance with living. We are able to live continuously in the expanded awareness that incorporates the knowledge of who we are beyond the ego, beyond death, beyond annihilation, and beyond the "unknown."

TAKING DEATH AS AN ADVISOR

My father died recently, and for the past several years I noticed that talking and reminiscing about the time he spent in the service during World War II was about the only thing he really wanted to do. When he told stories about the war years, he became really animated and enlivened, and his spirit shone in a most remarkable way, even though the war had been over for more than 50 years. He had spent the entire duration of the war, six years in all and the best part of his twenties, as an officer in the army engineers.

Now I knew that the war had taken its toll on him. As I was growing up, I watched the way his old emotional wounds gave him trouble and how the Post Traumatic Stress Syndrome that had remained untreated for so long affected his moods and his productivity. I saw, too, that he had a war inside himself, as he fought to keep the pain and sadness at bay so that he could have a life.

Thus it was that one day a couple of months before he died my curiosity got the better of me, and I pointed out to him the dichotomy of what I saw. I asked him how it was that he could get so involved in something that had happened so long ago and that must have been so traumatic. He pondered deeply for just a moment and then gave me the reply I had already half anticipated, but had wanted to hear from his own lips. He told me, in his own words, that it was only during those war years that he had felt completely present with life, even though he was living with death every moment of every day, and was fully conscious of that fact. Yet life on the edge of death was so challenging and exhilarating, he explained, and he was so connected to himself in every way, so sharp, energized, and aware, that he knew he was completely alive.

While I don't think that we necessarily need to live through a six-year war to bring us to a full life, the principle that the story reflects holds good. It was Don Juan, Carlos Castaneda's mystical teacher and one of my own guides, who taught that we must take death as an advisor—that when we live with an awareness that death could overtake us at any time and fully let that realization in and accept it, our life becomes more real and fulfilling. So too, will we, as we face life's challenges full on, with death as our advisor, become completely alive.

Using this key over time will bring us to a place of witnessing all of our fears, one by one. Even if we are never able to let go of each and every one of them, we will find ourselves becoming increasingly courageous about overriding them. After all, fear is just a frequency, like everything else in creation. Knowing this may be enough to open the dimensional doorways and to release the kundalini along its pathway of light to the crown.

A PROCESS

The following egoic clearing technique is called a "triangle" and is explained in more detail in *The Marriage of Spirit—Enlightened Living in Today's World.*

Draw a triangle in your journal. On the left side of the baseline, write "death," and on the right side of the baseline, write "life." The triangle technique is about trying to find the word that fits at the apex of the triangle. We call that word the "ascended balance;" it is a word that reconciles the polarity written at the baseline. The ascended balance word lifts our consciousness into the upper chakras, into a more unified state. At a mental-emotional level, finding the ascended balance word helps raise the kundalini toward the crown chakra. What word does that for you? In this instance you might use the word "detachment" or "eternality" or "equanimity." Accepting life and death with detachment allows the kundalini to ascend from the root chakra toward the crown. Often the word will come to you through feeling and intuition during meditation or quiet contemplation. Then, offer up the triangle with a prayer, like you did with the polarity and square techniques.

A PRAYER

Oh Eternity, I offer up the egoic imbalances, attractions, and repulsions toward life and death. Please bring me into a place of detachment and equanimity so that I may be made whole. I give thanks knowing this will be so. I accept my death.

A Meditation

Sit comfortably, with your spine upright but without strain, and take several deep, relaxing breaths. Allow your attention to let go into the luminous core within and feel the quality of expansion in that "I am" presence. As you gently focus your awareness on your core, allow that sense of "I am" to become more complete. Allow it to expand into the experience of being both nothing and everything, simultaneously. Invite and allow the ego to experience that it is nothing (no one thing). In that understanding comes the experience of actually being everything. That is liberation! Life and all of the things of this earth are by their very nature impermanent. Your essence, your being, is both eternal and all encompassing. Hold that experience of being both nothing and everything, as your attention stays gently centered in the core.

THE
SEVENTH KEY

ACCEPT
YOUR
DIVINITY

THIS KEY, THE SEVENTH, IS ABOUT LEARNING TO ACCEPT YOURSELF AS A MANIFESTATION OF UNIVERSAL PRESENCE, moving ultimately to the realization of yourself as one with the divine Self. Preparation for this step means being able to see and witness the ego through impersonal eyes to where you know that you are much more than the ego and that you exist beyond the boundaries of your personality.

Just below the crown chakra, there is a lock where we experience the doubt that we are divine. As we use this key, reaffirming and accepting our divinity, we dispel the doubt and open the lock. The flow of kundalini then moves up into the crown, and we come into the knowledge of who we truly are, reconnecting with our divine essence.

The shadow of doubt is the first sign that a crack has appeared in the seamless nature of existence—the unified state that is our ground of being. With the impulse to buy into the reality of the doubt, we are immediately split into our dual nature and are subject once again to the spin of all the polarities. If one learns to witness those moments of doubt, or self-doubt, to catch them in the moment that they happen, and to see them as illusory programming, it is possible not to "fall" into the spiral of egoic programming and the limited personality.

RETURNING TO ONENESS

The completion of our evolutionary cycle in this world begins when the realization dawns that we are not the ego, but that we are in fact the eternal Self. Life in the ego, with its transitory manifestation of boundaries and false appearances, is simply an expression of the temporary form taken for the journey through time and space. We become capable of seeing that this ephemeral world and all of its attributes, such as time, space, and duality, are simply a dream held in the unfathomable intelligence of existence. With the knowledge that our life is also a dream, with us in the starring role, we come to know ourselves also as the dreamer of the dream.

We have come to this world to play and learn lessons. Our time here is finished only when we awaken fully to the truth of "who we are" through every fiber of our being. When it is over, we will move on to another manifestation in some other world on some other dimensional plane, or perhaps we will return here to share our knowledge with others. If not, we will go home, merging permanently back into the Oneness, never to incarnate again.

GOING HOME

Samadhi is the Sanskrit word for the state known as unity consciousness or Oneness. It is the state we reclaim and enter more and more consciously as we return to knowledge of our divine origin. Unity consciousness is and has always been present with us, though usually relegated to the background of our awareness. It remains unseen as we focus intently on worldly distractions. Learning first to recognize samadhi and then to incorporate the vastness and eternality of samadhi into the limited bandwidth of separation is ascension. With the gradual spiritualizing of one's consciousness, the dawning of samadhi is a natural evolutionary occurrence.

There are many levels or intensities of samadhi. The entry into this state usually comes in gradually, although there can be peak experiences of it accompanied by a falling back into everyday consciousness for a while, before it becomes established permanently. The breakthrough moments with samadhi are more likely to happen if one works with a teacher who is always in samadhi.

The permanent return to Oneness happens when we

completely dissolve the old third-dimensional ego and pass through the eye of the needle, shifting from one dimension to another. When the final dissolution of the egoic identity happens like this, it is known as *Nirvikalpa* samadhi, which can last for varying lengths of time, from a few seconds to several months. When Nirvikalpa samadhi lasts for even a few hours, one returns from the experience retaining the awareness that one is not the separate ego, the separate personality, or even a separate, particularized being at all. The length of this absorption into the unmanifest decides how deeply the knowledge of Self is instituted in the awareness. This kind of samadhi is experienced sitting or lying down. It is not possible to function physically while it takes place, without coming out of it. It may take many experiences of Nirvikalpa samadhi to dissolve the separate state completely.

When all of the old ego has dissolved and the knowledge of Self is completely instituted, the samadhi state will remain as permanent. We then learn to live again in the world, fully functional and yet with the knowledge of being nothing but pure awareness. We live then with the clear sense of the Truth that we don't exist—in the old perceived way—that in fact nothing exists as it had seemed to in the old way. Our perception of reality has changed forever. We know that our illusory physical form is only an appearance and that it is fully multidimensional—even if the body still appears to be manifesting visibly in this world. Yet paradoxically, we live in samadhi and in a body in the world. This state is known as *Sahaja* samadhi.

Becoming multidimensional does not necessarily mean leaving this world. This physical world is not a third-dimensional world exclusively. It supports bodies that are held in Oneness and multidimensional consciousness just as easily.

There is another way in which we return to the Oneness, or return home, as people love to say. This is when we die physically. When the body dies, we transition out of this world, merging for a time into unity consciousness, the clear light of the unmanifest. This merging takes place for varying lengths of time, depending on how we have lived life. The merging could be just a split second or much longer. After it completes, we become conscious of, manifest a form on, and live for a time on another dimensional level—what in this world we call one of the heavenly realms. Again, this level is determined by how we have lived life. This is where we rest to review and learn the lessons that we missed here on earth. We may linger in the chosen world for quite awhile before the soul makes the choice to move into physical incarnation again.

Spiritual development taken to the point of samadhi is essentially a way of training for the death experience. The individual learns to let go, to transcend the fears that bind the ego and to allow dissolution to take place. Over time there are repeated experiences of samadhi, which mean passing through the veils of consciousness that hold separation in place. The entry into the Oneness, which is samadhi, renders the veils of ego increasingly transparent. With that transparency, eventually, we experience manifest creation and the unmanifest simultaneously, as one seamless, congruent reality.

Nothing truly exists except energy and consciousness. All worlds are transitory and ephemeral—the play of light. Even the higher dimensional worlds exist as virtual realities, expressed from the endless dreaming of the unmanifest. We may pass through them for a while, but eventually we will return to the Oneness for all eternity.

As we use this key, we encounter deep-seated commitments and contracts that we made with higher consciousness before we incarnated. They are contracts in which we agreed to live within the parameters of the separate state and within the limited bandwidth of this world, to complete the lessons we came here for. Once we realize consciously that we have made these agreements, it is necessary to consider rescinding them and to make the choice to void them out. No real and permanent change can take place until we have dissolved the contracts and agreements we made to play the game of life in the third dimension. It is necessary to make a statement to Spirit that you no longer wish to live in the separate state or be bound by the limitation that it demands of you. If you are determined to make the journey of ascension, then the contracts will be dissolved.

Signing the contract to live disconnected from divine knowledge of who we truly are, is for most people a necessity for being born into this world. We chose to come into this world to have the experiences it provides and to learn the lessons that a life lived in separation and limitation can teach us.

Take the time to review your life, and realize how you have benefited, how much you have grown, and how the ego's strengths and weaknesses have been shown to you as your life has unfolded, allowing growth. If you are reading this, then you have made some headway toward breaking out of the box of third-dimensional awareness, rising to meet the challenges of limitation and growing to see through the illusion of your mind with all its strengths and weaknesses. Like the prodigal child, you are on your way home, and you will be welcomed royally.

This world with its extremes of dualistic dark and light is a ripe place to grow and develop. It allows us to see all the heavens and hells, all the negatives and positives. It is an unusual world in its polarization of dark and light and in its juxtaposition of good and evil. These states also manifest in the other dimensional worlds but in different combinations. Nowhere is there a world quite like this one, where the two are so perfectly juxtaposed and well defined, allowing us to see the Truth in the illusion. The Earth is unique in all the universe in this way, and it offers us a wonderful way to see what it takes to find our way home.

As we enter this world with its freedom of choice and freedom of will, we get the opportunity to review where we are in our evolutionary journey toward higher consciousness. Do we still confuse the egoic light and dark with the Truth? Planet earth is a great place to learn to distinguish between them, and to choose where we want to be positioned, in the battle between good and evil. It is a wondrously easy place to come to know our destiny.

This world is a perfect place to find our enlightenment. Being here allows us to choose to see through the illusion of good and evil. We can choose to let go of it completely as we return directly to source.

A DEEPER SAMADHI

Recently I found a journal entry dated December of 1986, two years before I experienced final dissolution into Oneness. Moving into Nirvikalpa samadhi was about to begin. The journal entry was an experience of a "lower" samadhi, *Salvikalpa* samadhi. You will see as you read it that there is a "residue" of a subject-object separation between me and Universal Mind still evident. I have taken the liberty of including it without much editing to keep the transmission and immediacy of the experience intact. Even though you will read this in a few minutes, for me hours elapsed between writing sentences. Using it here is a way of illustrating the experience of dissolution and the resulting shift in perception that happens. I was already fairly deep into the meditation when I realized that I needed to document it, something I had never done before. So I went to the typewriter and began typing it with my eyes closed, so that I could stay immersed in it.

This was the night I began my journey to an inter-dimensional state. This night I slipped through the eye of the needle into the fourth dimension. Afterwards I realized why I had needed to type it as it happened— because re-reading it took me right back into the experience, and for several months helped to ground the new state in conscious awareness forever. Perhaps there was another reason. Could it be that I was always planning to share the knowledge it contains, with you? If you read this slowly, you may be able to feel into the state that I was in when I wrote it.

JOURNAL ENTRY ABOUT SAMADHI, DECEMBER 1986
A question came up in my evening meditation today. It was this—what is love? The answer came resounding through to my awareness—there is nothing that is not love! As I type this I see that love is the substance and energy of existence. The floor, the chairs in the room

that I see, and even everything that I can think of, is love. As I penetrate to the depth of my awareness with the question, I can feel the underlying 'sameness' of all of the vast diversity of life. Its essential core energy is cohesively and unmistakably the same stuff—love. That's all there is.

Let me describe it. I am typing slowly with my eyes closed as I plumb this new state and try to find words for it. Firstly, it is support, or supportiveness and fullness. It is inter-dimensional, transcending life, death, separation, time and space, and yet it is also beyond all dimensions. It knows no boundaries—either of skin, mind, or structured solidity. It is permeable, interpenetrating and simultaneously 'all-where.' It is complete reverence, perfection, and changelessness, yet is able to contain all change and all diversity within it.

Calling it love seems natural as it seemingly has its origin in the heart. My perception is of it flowing from there. This new reality is definitely the new system of the heart (new for me). It allows everything, on examination, to seem perfectly okay. Conflicts, if they were there, would only be light disagreements, not of much consequence. In fact the diversity we see in this world and which arises from the sameness, would be known by us as the joyous manifestation of the whimsy of creation. Variety that has no purpose other than truly just for spicing up our lives—just for the fun of it. It occurs to me that it would never be for killing or destruction and definitely not for the purpose of spending large sums of money on the equipment of destruction.

What of comparing and competition? The question is directed at this new me. The answer: There would be gamesmanship and fun—sports for interaction. Could there be war here? It hardly feels likely. As I sit here with the question I see that the war in me is over. In this experience I'm so connected to the chairs, the table, and the sofa. If someone walked into the room, I'd be as close to them as I am to all of myself. They would be completely present in my awareness. I'd know them as love too.

And what of fear, I ask? The answer: As your awareness field slides up and down, so do you fortunes. We cannot know what will happen tomorrow. It depends on the level of your attention. I understand this to mean I am in transition between levels. I am aware that the attention of a human is rather like an elevator. Each of the floors is a different plane of awareness or dimension. It takes energy to power the elevator and wherever the elevator sits, is the determining factor of our destiny.

This experience appears to open a new dimension of being for me—a new paradigm of perception. It is supercharged 'Here and Now.' Verbalizing it strengthens it enormously. As that happens, I would say that I'm in the unified field. This state is the interconnectedness of all of existence, omnipresent, omnipotent, omniscient being. It's so real—it's my reality, right here and now, in the room.

I reflect on the fact that the unified field has been called many things by many different people. It is the all-encompassing ocean of existence, an ocean shiny with light. At times for me, sitting here in front of my type-writer, everything stops in timelessness and the energy feels like an endless wave that never breaks. It rolls in continuously. It's a flow, a current, a river. Although paradoxically, it never actually moves—it just seems to. It shimmers and vibrates. I see that it is always present with me. Even when there is activity and action—it just becomes obscured by the action. But if the activity stops, the flow returns. I know now that the infinite ocean never leaves us, we simply become distracted by activity and forget where we started—how we started. I stop typing, and here it is again! The flow has returned—or rather I have returned to it. I return to typing, and right now typing is barely obscuring it.

This experience came about just from me asking about love! Love! It was that one word that was the catalyst. I have done so much processing work understanding consciousness, that I assume that the work and the question just exploded into a new paradigm of perception- -a new reality—one of unity and synthesis rather than of separation and division.

There is no body here at the moment, just energy

and flow filling the room. Seen and felt. Occasionally some sort of thought or desire arises and I recognize it as my personal self. I let it go by, not able to hold onto it. I have no need for identity right now.

A moment of whimsy comes offering a symbol. The awareness field filling my mind looks like concentric hearts. Imagine that you dropped a pebble into a pond and that it made heart-shaped ripples that flowed out infinitely. This is what I am seeing in my mind.

This new heart awareness is so ecstatic that I will be happy to sit here and meditate all night. As I register my love for it, the energy field intensifies tenfold. Opening my eyes, I see the objects in the room begin to disintegrate in a brilliant white light, and I am drawn more completely away from the appearance of the world and deeper into undifferentiated consciousness.

Luckily, even as I sit and type these words with my eyes closed, enjoying the flow of luminosity in the meditation, the immediacy of the experience is not lost at all. I sense Uma, the Divine Mother. She is walking in the garden of my heart. Her presence lifts my awareness into the unified field. This is a rainbow world. Her heart blazes through mine like a huge mandala in my chest. It is a living, moving thing that unfurls, radiates, vibrates, and then melts. Lately, I have been aware that she has held my heart night and day without fail, for lifetimes.

I can attest to my awareness no longer traveling

through the labyrinth of my mind. Awareness has chosen the freedom of the flow. As the thoughts cease, the flow of light is channeled through and into the body. In this moment I wish only to release the body as a limitation—and as I wish it, it relaxes. I'm free—awareness soars like a bird. Something in me marvels momentarily. Is this a wild journey or what? Certainly it is a journey into increasingly subtle states of Universal Mind. Prophetically I know that this freedom is, in itself, a new frontier for me. The intensity will, in time, reveal its subtlety as another land, another dimension. Its particulars will be entered and unraveled later, I feel. These are experiences that cannot be talked about—only known.

Support from the invisible realms has made the journey possible. The fact that I can be taken by Universal Mind and Mother into uncharted territory, beyond my understanding, and be given the understandings that divine mind is showing me is amazing. Only by being merged with this Universal Mind can I face and experience the unknown, beyond my old self. This is the mind where we create all possible futures and pasts and divulge our own knowledge to ourselves. It is a place where one can drink in the diversity of existence at its source. All of being is revealed here. This journey has its beginning and end in the heart—love and genesis.

Moving deeper into the heart, the frequency is rose colored and it speaks to me of being loved deeply by the

Source. But now subject and object are merging, so I must talk of being the one who is also doing the loving. Surrender is the quality of being here. It is the place where there are no secrets and no separations. Here there is no leeway for anything but 'That Which Is'— where there is nothing but Truth, where I am the experience itself, before the 'experiencer' has been split off and separated.

Merging with the Infinite Heart, I become one with a vast land of heart-centeredness that stretches 'all-where' and has no boundaries. It seems to be at the core of everything. There is no separation between the Divine and me, nor indeed between anything, in this unity.

I am inside Mother's being. It is an awareness field that has no boundaries. There is no thought, just a knowing that this is how it is at the Source. The Mother's boundlessness has made it safe for me to become my own Source, which is also the Source of everything. The inner core, my inner core, is everywhere at once. The experience of this defies description really. It is paradoxical, because the experience is beyond relativity and our language is governed and conceived in states of time and space. This is a 'Reality' experience, instead of a relativity experience.

My heart has always been here. I know this now. But I have not been aware of it before. There have been distractions, worldly matters, and conditioned attitudes and concepts that have blocked this seeing. Slowly over the years, I have examined the belief systems that I was conditioned into, and allowed them to dissolve as I saw where they were inadequate and too painful to live with. It seems that as they have now dissolved almost completely, I have come to the 'base coat' as it were, the very core and ground of being that is left.

This is a new system, a new paradigm, a totally new way of perceiving everything. I am enthralled by the understanding that it was there all the time, behind the belief systems and the old description of the world that I was given as a child and human being, resident on planet earth.

A PROCESS

Do a square to help unlock any doubt you may have of your divinity.

Make four lists:

The desire to accept your divinity
The fear of accepting your divinity
The desire to doubt your divinity
The fear of doubting your divinity

Offer up the list with a prayer.

A PRAYER

Oh Eternity, I offer up my egoic desires and fears of accepting and doubting my divinity. Please bring me into balance and make me conscious of myself as a manifestation of the universal presence. I accept my divinity.

A MEDITATION

As with the others, begin this meditation by sitting up comfortably and by breathing deeply to relax into a state of restful alertness. Visualize the core as a luminous fluorescent tube running down the center of your subtle body, slightly in front of your spine, and feel its presence. Sit with your attention on the core, and allow yourself to become very still and centered. Now bring your awareness up to the sixth chakra, the third eye, which is between the eyebrows and slightly above. Stay here for a few moments to feel the quality of the energy of this chakra. Now bring your attention several inches back to an area right in the middle of your skull, located directly between your ears and behind the third eye. This is the *cave of Brahman*. Gently hold your attention in this area, and as you do so, you will feel your awareness expand and become even more luminous. You may also feel that you are firmly established at the center of the cosmos, and with that comes a sense of the steady, even flow of divine energy of which you are an integral part. After spending some time focused here, allow your awareness to move up and out from that spot—opening your crown chakra and allowing an even greater sense of divine flow. Let the flow of light and energy pour down into and move up out of your subtle body. As you continue to sit, hold your crown chakra open, from the cave of Brahman, and allow yourself to experience the exquisite perfection of your divine nature. In doing so, know that this is who and what you truly are.

SHIFTING DIMENSIONS

So far we have focused our exploration of the evolution of human conscious-ness mainly on moving from the third dimension to the fourth, from a paradigm of power-oriented consciousness to a paradigm of heart-centered consciousness.

As you may have gathered by now, when enough people on the planet hold their consciousness primarily in a certain chakra, the planet experiences an era or epoch defined by the consciousness and qualities associated with that chakra. The early humans who were hunter-gatherers lived in a paradigm associated with survival, which is the root chakra. The next era was associated with the second chakra, and was about fertility and controlling our survival by growing crops. The next era, the third dimension, in which we are now living, is associated with the third chakra and is about power issues—to develop personal power and especially to learn lessons about the abuse of power.

The next era, the fourth dimension, will be a paradigm of heart-centeredness, and it is associated with the fourth chakra. Humanity's collective ascension process is its evolutionary path through the chakra levels. We will eventually evolve into the fifth dimension and beyond.

As individuals, we do not have to wait thousands of years and hundreds of lifetimes for a new era in order to move into higher dimensions. We can each make a personal evolutionary journey if we want it. We can ascend into the higher dimensions in this lifetime if we are willing to do the work necessary to transform.

Most people on the planet are in third-dimensional consciousness right now and since the planet is moving up in its evolution, everyone must move as well. We are moving into fourth-dimensional consciousness. A fairly accurate analogy of this process is to view the ego as though it were an onion. As we process and use the seven keys, our consciousness ascends through the core from root to crown. Every time we experience that complete movement from root to crown by opening the seven locks, we peel layers of our egoic onion. This is the clearing process. Every time we make that kundalini–ascension journey from root to crown, more onion layers peel away, and we are closer to the pure, pristine experience of the core. Thus we are gradually moving into fourth-dimensional consciousness. Eventually, we peel away all of the onion layers associated with third-dimensional egoic consciousness until we have reached the core, and we shift, becoming firmly established in fourth-dimensional consciousness. Many people who are on a spiritual path now are somewhere between the two, with a foot in each dimension.

Once we are complete with the third dimension, have peeled all its layers, have learned all its lessons, and are established in the fourth dimension, we begin to work on a whole new onion. There is a fourth-dimensional onion to clear. We process and can use the seven keys in our continuing ascension toward the fifth dimension. When we finish with the fourth dimension, there is a fifth dimensional onion to clear, and so forth.

Here is an analogy for the ascension process. It is as though we are standing on the third floor of a multi-story building. Above us is a trapdoor in the ceiling that opens up to the next floor. When we have peeled all the layers of the third dimension and finished all our lessons there, we climb up through the trapdoor and can stand on the floor of the fourth story. Above us again is another trapdoor in the ceiling that allows us to access the fifth story after we have peeled all the layers of the fourth dimension.

The core is like a stepladder we can use to climb up through the trapdoors, or rather like an elevator shaft that can take us up story after story, as we finish with the lessons and experiences of each dimension. We can access each floor by processing our consciousness and by using the seven keys.

It is not within the scope of this book to describe the qualities of all of the higher dimensions, but each dimension has its own set of rules for the flow of energy.

In general, as we ascend to higher dimensions, we experience more connectedness or unity consciousness and less polarity. For example, as we move from the third dimension to the fourth dimension, we experience less of an us-and-them mentality and more equality; less prejudice and more acceptance and greater friendliness; less fear, paranoia, and suspicion and more tolerance and compassion. Since life will not be viewed from the narrow bandwidth of good–bad, right–wrong, there will be more receptivity to life and to other species. We will find ourselves able to see the intrinsic nature of all of life. As we ascend to higher dimensions, we come to live closer to the experience of pure essence, pure God-consciousness, our true Self. Eventually there is only Oneness, that which is.

We have a subtle energy body on every dimension, and so in a sense we are already operating on every dimension, although most people are not aware of this. This means that we have a vehicle to contain our awareness on each of the different dimensions. The act of shifting dimensions, or even temporarily traversing the dimensions, means waking up more completely to that part of us already living on that other dimension.

We are not disappearing into a void when we let go and allow a shift into the next dimension. Even though surrendering in this way may feel like the formless unknown, it is not "empty." What happens is that we let go of our current self and move into the path of light, the core, and travel, so to speak, up the elevator shaft, emerging in the next level. When we first arrive at the next level, our experience could be anything from a slightly dysfunctional feeling, to being as disoriented as a newborn baby.

You may experience strange symptoms such as extreme vulnerability at first, as well as states of joy and bliss as you use the keys and as you experience your consciousness passing through the dimensional doorways. In time we begin to wake up to ourselves, to the awareness we hold on the other dimensions.

JACOB'S LADDER —
THE ASCENSION GRID

There are energy grids in subtle consciousness, energetic lines which crisscross and surround our body and our planet, forming matrices of light. These grids each have different qualities and in general serve to support and uphold physical matter, planet earth, its life forms, and their evolution. On September 17, 2001, a few days after the two airplanes crashed into the World Trade Center, a new grid was turned on—ignited and activated for the first time.

Globally, everyone with commitments to the light was plugged into this new grid, or web, as some are calling it. Those with commitments to ascend were connected onto the grid at the precise place where they were able to reach and sustain their connection to it. In other words, the grid is fashioned rather like a ladder, forming a bridge that joins the old third-dimensional grid to the Christ-consciousness grid. Some call it a peace grid, or a golden grid, or a love grid. Ultimately, this grid is going to make it much easier for everyone to feel supported as they awaken out of the old paradigm of third-dimensional consciousness.

As of the writing of this book, the grid has been created and activated only enough to make it immediately usable. We have yet to learn how to use more fully the resource that it offers us. It is up to us to tend it, to build its strength and luminosity with our own strength and luminosity as we grow and ascend, and to increase its number of anchor points, both in our own bodies and backyards. It was anchored by many individuals at several significant places of spiritual power around the world, but as yet it remains somewhat delicate and not fully active. We can help to anchor it by asking inwardly in prayer and meditation for it to happen. The clearer we become by processing ourselves, the stronger our ability to connect to it, to access it, and to anchor it.

In what is one of Spirit's wonderful paradoxes, the new grid is both inside us and outside us at the same time. As we discussed in previous chapters, there is a direct correlation between the inside and the outside. Beyond the polarized perception of our conditioned mode of being, which is separation from every thing we see around us, our inside and our outside are really one and the same thing. By not defining ourselves as the physical body, we know intuitively that we are connected to everything on the outside. Learning to use the seven keys helps us to see beyond the polarity of inside and outside and will allow us to climb this ladder grid towards Oneness.

Built into the rocks in the grand gallery of the Great Pyramid of Gizeh, there is what some people interpret as a calendar. The calendar spans many centuries, and its timeline marks very specific dates throughout history, such as the birth of Christ and more recently World Wars I and II. Interestingly the calendar ended on September 17, 2001. Was it possibly meant to indicate "the end of the world?" Certainly it is safe to say that after the events of September 11, 2001, the world will never be the same again.

On the same day that the calendar in the pyramid ended, the grid was activated. That day, I was with a group of people on retreat. At noon we were in deep meditation and were taken through an initiation into higher-dimensional consciousness. As our meditation progressed, we used the seven keys in a guided meditation to move through the seven doorways. Just as we completed the journey, the river of light, the meridian at the center of the subtle body, the core, became activated for the whole group, glowing vigorously from everyone's root to crown, opening everyone's crown to a new level of clarity. The group had all been lifted up. There was so much love and luminosity flowing between everyone when we broke for lunch, that it was obvious we were actually functioning for the moment from the open heart—in a higher-vibratory paradigm.

During the meditation I was given a vision. I saw that the new grid had been turned on and that everyone choosing light had been connected to it. I saw, too, that in that moment, the population of the world was now divided by their choice. It had been split into two categories, those seeking the light and those who were not. These two groups are now held in parallel realities, instead of being meshed together as they were in the past. On September 17, 2001, some of the earth's population were placed on the new grid and some remained on the old.

In that moment of initiation, there was a splitting of the streams of evolution for humanity—a fork in the road had appeared for souls incarnating on planet earth. September 11, 2001, was the very loud drumroll heralding a wake-up call for humanity. And September 17, 2001, without much fanfare and in a manner subtle and imperceptible to most, marked a moment of initiation that was the end of the known world.

However, it is as yet not too late for someone to choose to move with the light stream. Of course, anyone who changes their commitment and is willing to do the personal transformation work can still hitch a ride into the higher vibratory paradigms.

It is likely that many of the souls choosing to move with the evolutionary stream into higher dimensions will flip-flop back and forth between the third dimension and the fourth or fifth for awhile. It is not usual for someone to shift all at once into the new paradigm. When we have a peak experience, we temporarily merge with the faster vibration, but often we have to go back to the old vibration and do more clearing work before we can permanently relocate to the new. This back-and-forth movement is quite normal and goes on for quite awhile.

GOING GOD-DIRECT

The new ascension grid offers a wonderful new opportunity for all who seek the light to accelerate their path of ascension into the Oneness. In addition to the ascension grid, there are many powerful tools coming forward, such as the seven keys and other processing techniques, to assist us on the journey of spiritual awakening. It is important to find tools that work for you and to use them regularly. Processing egoic consciousness is helpful, and even essential now, if you want to wake up. Also choosing to be on a fast path is helpful now.

In general just meditation or prayer or studying with a spiritual teacher is not enough in and of itself, with some exceptions of course. Spiritual seekers must use their initiative now more than ever before, to become conscious of the luminous core of enlightened awareness that is within each of us. A passive approach is not what is called for at this time of enormous change and acceleration. Simply waiting for grace to bop us on the head with a magic wand and wake us up is a very slow path. The opportunity to grow and evolve is greater now than perhaps ever before in the history of our planet, and we are being asked to meet Spirit halfway on this leg of the journey. To take an active role in processing the ego and in peeling its onion layers is a virtue beyond measure at this time. Moving beyond avoidance and denial of our shadow issues offers great rewards and is easier now than ever before. Spirit is offering special dispensations, so to speak, to those who are willing to heed this call. In other words, a little bit of processing goes a long way toward awakening, and there is an enormous amount of help and support from the invisible realms at the present time.

During this turbulent time of humanity's evolution, it is essential that we begin to look within for the answers. By clearing our own consciousness, by taking responsibility for our own life's situations, we move beyond victim consciousness, beyond loss, beyond blame and beyond apparent betrayals and powerlessness. We become capable of viewing the ego impersonally and moving into compassion, forgiveness, and non-dual truth. In this way we develop a very personal and real connection with our own inner divine self. A friend of mine coined a phrase for this path of ascension and returning to Oneness. It is called "going God-direct."

In a way, there has never been an easier time to wake up. The lessons are coming thick and fast as time seems to be speeding up. We are experiencing "instant karma," which is way of saying that cause and effect have speeded up: The consequences of our actions, or karmas, are quickly returned to us in the form of lessons so that we can finish with our business in the separate system.

If we work with the seven keys and process with each lesson, the neutral witness is strengthened. As the witness develops and strengthens, we are able moment by moment to maintain our conscious connection to the truth of who we are—that we are spirit: pure, eternal, timeless beings. As we become more consciously connected to the core, we see beyond duality, beyond the illusion of our separateness. Surrendering to divine will becomes easier and easier as we develop the God-direct connection.

The God-direct path is about accepting our own divinity. As we use the keys, or use any method of processing the limited ego that is pushed and pulled by its desires, fears, attractions, and repulsions, we ascend into that knowledge of our true Self. We return to the conscious awareness of that which we truly are and have always been—eternal Oneness.

ABOUT THE AUTHORS AND CoreLight

LESLIE TEMPLE-THURSTON was born in South Africa and graduated from the University of Witwatersrand, Johannesburg, with a bachelor's degree in fine arts. With the gift of clairaudience, she was urged by her inner guidance to emigrate during the height of apartheid. In the mid-1970s she moved to the United States with her family. Here she deepened her studies of ancient wisdom through meditation and yogic teachings, and explored the works of the new spiritual psychologies.

In the late 1980s after many years of a transformational inner journey, she experienced a complete dissolution of her old identity and a profound spiritual awakening. With this came the gift of being able to share through her gaze, her hands, and her voice a transmission of grace, unconditional love, and healing energy.

Since 1988, Leslie has been a mentor and guide to hundreds of spiritual seekers worldwide. Today she continues to offer events throughout the United States,

South Africa, and other countries and is dedicated to working closely with groups of people who are committed to transformation and spiritual awakening. She is also the author of *The Marriage of Spirit—Enlightened Living in Today's World*. Her extensive teachings are available on audiotape and videotape through CoreLight.

BRAD LAUGHLIN is the Executive Director of the non-profit organization, CoreLight, which presents seminars on the seven keys, *The Marriage of Spirit*, and offers other transformational events. Brad is a spiritual mentor and travels extensively worldwide leading sacred site tours. He is the co-author of *The Marriage of Spirit— Enlightened Living in Today's World*. He has a BS degree from Duke University and lives in Santa Fe, New Mexico.

CORELIGHT is a non-profit organization dedicated to assisting people on the path of transformation and Self-discovery and to fostering inner and outer peace in the world. The name, CoreLight, refers to the luminous core of enlightenment within each one of us.

CoreLight offers public events and ongoing courses with Leslie Temple-Thurston: Spiritual Warrior Training is a correspondence course via audiotape, books, and the Internet. Teacher Training is a correspondence course as well and includes bi-annual gatherings. For a schedule of Leslie's public events or information about the courses, please contact CoreLight.

CoreLight also offers guided meditation CDs, books, videotapes, and audiotapes of Leslie's teachings on an extensive range of topics, all of which are available by catalog and via our website. Please contact us for the free catalog.

CoreLight

223 North Guadalupe Street, PMB 275
Santa Fe, NM 87501-1850

888-989-3552 (toll-free U.S./Canada)
505-424-8844 (outside U.S./Canada)
505-424-8848 (fax)
www.corelight.org
info@corelight.org

THE MARRIAGE OF SPIRIT — ENLIGHTENED LIVING IN TODAY'S WORLD

by Leslie Temple-Thurston
with Brad Laughlin

ISBN 0-9660182-0-6 • $22.88 hardcover
Sample chapters available online at
www.marriageofspirit.com

The Marriage of Spirit is a hand-
book for spiritual awakening while
living and working in the world.
Rooted in the ancient principle
of the unification of opposites,
it offers simple, powerful, and
fast exercises, which accelerate
the path to experiencing divine
presence in our lives. By balancing our consciousness through

using these techniques, we become very
practical, grounded, and functional in the world. In this
groundbreaking book, Leslie Temple-Thurston shares
the story of the awakenings that led to her spiritual
transformation, and her eclectic, yogic-influenced
approach to western enlightenment.

"Integrating the multitude of physical, mental, and emotional experiences of modern life may be a difficult undertaking, but this beautiful book offers a way through the confusion. Based on Temple-Thurston's transformational workshops, *The Marriage of Spirit* combines modern psychological techniques with ancient wisdom practices..."

—The Institute of
Noetic Sciences

"...incorporating ancient sources from Taoism to Gnosticism, the philosophy and techniques presented here...are explained in compassionate detail."

—NAPRA Review

"[A book that is] calm and clear, and should be welcome to many spiritual seekers. Recommended."

—Library Journal

*The Marriage of Spirit is available
in bookstores or through*
CoreLight Publishing
223 North Guadalupe Street, PMB 275
Santa Fe, NM 87501-1850

(888) 989-3552 (toll-free U.S./Canada)
(505) 424-8844 (outside U.S./Canada)
505-424-8848 (fax)
Website: www.corelight.org
email: info@corelight.org